Everyman, I will go with thee,
and be thy guide

THE EVERYMAN
LIBRARY

*The Everyman Library was founded by J. M. Dent
in 1906. He chose the name Everyman because he wanted
to make available the best books ever written in every
field to the greatest number of people at the cheapest possible
price. He began with Boswell's 'Life of Johnson';
his one-thousandth title was Aristotle's 'Metaphysics',
by which time sales exceeded forty million.*

*Today Everyman paperbacks remain true to
J. M. Dent's aims and high standards, with a wide range
of titles at affordable prices in editions which address
the needs of today's readers. Each new text is reset to give
a clear, elegant page and to incorporate the latest thinking
and scholarship. Each book carries the pilgrim logo,
the character in 'Everyman', a medieval morality play,
a proud link between Everyman
past and present.*

H. G. Wells

THE ISLAND OF DOCTOR MOREAU

Edited by
BRIAN ALDISS

EVERYMAN
J. M. DENT · LONDON
CHARLES E. TUTTLE
VERMONT

Introduction and other critical apparatus
© J. M. Dent, 1993

Text copyright by the Literary Executors
of the Estate of H. G. Wells 1993

Chronology compiled by John Lawton 1993

First published in Everyman Paperbacks in 1993
Reprinted 1994, 1995, 1996 (twice), 1997, 1999

J. M. Dent Ltd
Orion Publishing Group
Orion House
5 Upper St Martin's Lane, London WC2H 9EA
and
Charles E. Tuttle Co. Inc.
28 South Main Street, Rutland, Vermont
05701, USA

Made in Great Britain by
The Guernsey Press Co. Ltd, Guernsey, Channel Islands

British Library Cataloguing-in-Publication Data
is available upon request.

ISBN 0 460 87258 3

CONTENTS

NOTE ON THE AUTHOR AND EDITOR

H. G. WELLS was born in Bromley, Kent in 1866. After working as a draper's apprentice and pupil-teacher, he won a scholarship to the Normal School of Science, South Kensington, in 1884, studying under T. H. Huxley. He was awarded a first-class honours degree in biology and resumed teaching, but had to retire after a kick from an ill-natured pupil, at football, afflicted his kidneys. He worked in poverty in London as a crammer while experimenting in journalism and stories, and published textbooks on biology and physiography (1893), but it was *The Time Machine* (1895) that launched his literary career. Many scientific romances and short stories began to be paralleled with sociological and political books and tracts, notably *Anticipations* (1901), *Mankind in the Making* (1903), *A Modern Utopia* (1905). His full-length, largely autobiographical novels began with *Love and Mr Lewisham* (1900), *Kipps* (1905), *Tono-Bungay* and *Ann Veronica* (1909), the last promoting the outspoken, socially and sexually liberated 'New Woman'. He married his cousin Isabel in 1891, but later eloped with, and subsequently married, Catherine Robbins, 'Jane'. A constant philanderer, he invited scandal by including his lightly concealed private affairs in *Ann Veronica* and *The New Machiavelli* (1911). Shaw and the Webbs had invited him into the Fabian Society and soon regretted it. Wells increasingly used fiction as a platform for the ideas and visions of a world-state which preoccupied him, but he foresaw that the novel itself would decline to be replaced by candid autobiography. After about 1920, critical attention was turning towards his natural successor Aldous Huxley and the 'pure' non-journalistic novels of James Joyce and Virginia Woolf. His mass public dwindled, though it welcomed *The Outline of History*, of that year, and long continued to do so. The Second World War and the cataclysm of Hiroshima confirmed the pessimism which had throughout accompanied his exuberant hopes and visions. His last book was titled, with some personal significance, *Mind at the End of its Tether* (1945), but his vigour continued almost to his death in 1946. In his last two decades he had produced some forty books.

BRIAN ALDISS has recently published his autobiography, *The Twinkling of an Eye*. His Squire Quartet is being reprinted in a uniform edition in Abacus paperback. His long utopian novel, written in collaboration with Sir Roger Penrose, *White Mars* is with the publisher. Aldiss is a Fellow of the Royal Society of Literature and former President of World SF, as well as Vice-President of the H. G. Wells Society. His history of science fiction, *Trillion Year Spree*, with David Wingrove, is a standard authority on its subject.

NOTE ON THE TEXT

The text reprinted here is that of the first edition of *The Island of Doctor Moreau* published in 1896 by William Heinemann.

CHRONOLOGY OF WELLS'S LIFE

Year	Age	Life
1866		Born 21 September, Bromley, Kent, to a working class family: father a gardener, shopkeeper and cricketer; mother a maid and housekeeper
1873	7	Entered Thomas Morley's Bromley Academy

CHRONOLOGY OF HIS TIMES

Year	Arts & Science	History & Politics
1865	Mendel's *Law of Heredity*	End of American Civil War; Lincoln assassinated
1866	Dostoevsky's *Crime and Punishment*	Russia defeated Austria at Sadowa
1867	Ibsen's *Peer Gynt*; Lister experiments with sterile surgery	Dominion of Canada founded
1868	Browning's *The Ring and the Book*; typewriter first patented	Gladstone Prime Minister
1869	Jules Verne's *20,000 Leagues Under the Sea*; Flaubert's *Education Sentimentale*; John Stuart Mill's *On the Subjection of Women*	Suez Canal opened
1870	Charles Dickens dies; T. H. Huxley's *Theory of Biogenesis*	Franco-Prussian War; Prussia defeats France at Sedan; fall of Napoleon III; Education Act, introducing elementary education for 5–13 year olds
1871	Lewis Carroll's *Alice Through the Looking Glass*; George Eliot's *Middlemarch*; Charles Darwin's *The Descent of Man*	Paris Commune suppressed; the Chicago Fire; unification of Germany
1872	Edison's duplex telegraph	The Secret Ballot Act
1873	Tolstoy's *Anna Karenina*; James Clarke Maxwell's *Electricity and Magnetism*	Napoleon III dies in exile in Kent; David Livingstone dies in what is now Zambia
1874	Thomas Hardy's *Far from the Madding Crowd*; First Impressionist exhibition in Paris	Disraeli Prime Minister; Factory Act introduces fifty-six-and-a-half hour week
1875	Bizet's *Carmen*	London Medical School for Women founded
1876	Alexander Graham Bell's telephone; Twain's *Tom Sawyer*	Battle of Little Bighorn; death of General Custer; Queen Victoria becomes Empress of India

Year	Age	Life
1880	14	Apprenticed to Rodgers and Benyer, Drapers, at Windsor
1881	15	Pupil-teacher at Alfred Williams' school at Wookey, Somerset; pupil at Midhurst Grammar School; apprenticed to Southsea Drapery Emporium
1882		
1883–4		Under-master at Midhurst Grammar School; wins scholarship and bursary at Normal School of Science, South Kensington
1884–7		Studies under T. H. Huxley at the Normal School of Science; begins to write; first published work appears in May 1887 in the *Science Schools Journal* – *A Tale of the Twentieth Century*
1887	20	Teacher at Holt Academy, Wrexham
1888	22	Returns to London after illness, working as a teacher; *The Chronic Argonauts* published in *Science Schools Journal*
1890	24	B.Sci degree
1891	25	Tutor for University Correspondence College; marries his cousin, Isabel Wells; *The Rediscovery of the Unique* published in the *Fortnightly Review*

Year	Arts & Science	History & Politics
1877	Thomas Edison's phonograph	Britain annexes the Transvaal
1879	Dostoevsky's *The Brothers Karamazov*	Zulu Wars, South Africa
1880	Electric light devised by T. A. Edison (USA) and by J. W. Swan (Scotland)	Boer uprising in the Transvaal
1881	Henry James's *Portrait of a Lady*	President Garfield murdered, USA
1882	R. L. Stevenson's *Treasure Island*	Married Woman's Property Act
1883	Death of Karl Marx; William Thomson (later, Lord Kelvin) publishes *On the Size of Atoms*; first skyscraper in Chicago	Fabian Society founded
1884	Twain's *Huckleberry Finn*; invention of Maxim machine gun	Berlin Conference on division of Africa; Gladstone's Reform Act extends vote to country householders
1885	Zola's *Germinal*; Pasteur's vaccine to cure hydrophobia; Karl Benz's automobile	Battle of Khartoum; Death of General Gordon
1886	R. L. Stevenson's *Dr Jekyll and Mr Hyde*; Rimbaud's *Les Illuminations*	Lord Salisbury Prime Minister
1887	H. W. Goodwin's celluloid film invented; speed of light measured	Queen Victoria's Golden Jubilee
1888	Kipling's *Plain Tales from the Hills*; Eastman's box camera; Dunlop's pneumatic tyre; Hertz discovers electromagnetic waves	Kaiser Frederick III dies after only three months as Emperor of Germany; accession of Wilhelm II
1889	Death of Robert Browning; T. H. Huxley's *Agnosticism*; Eiffel Tower built	Archduke Rudolf, heir to the Emperor, commits suicide at Mayerling, Austria
1890	Emily Dickinson's *Poems*; discovery of tetanus and diptheria viruses	Bismarck dismissed by the Kaiser; the 'O'Shea' scandal; Charles Parnell resigns as leader of Irish party
1891	Wilde's *The Picture of Dorian Gray*; Hardy's *Tess of the D'Urbervilles*	

Year	Age	Life
1892	26	Meets Amy Catherine Robbins – 'Jane'
1893	27	Elopes with Jane; in poor health; first published book, *A Text Book of Biology*; lives by writing for the rest of his life
1895	29	Marries Jane; they settle in Woking; meets George Bernard Shaw; *The Time Machine*; *Select Conversations with an Uncle*; *The Wonderful Visit*; *The Stolen Bacillus and Other Incidents*
1896	30	*The Island of Doctor Moreau*; *The Wheels of Chance*; meets George Gissing
1897	31	*The Invisible Man*; *The Plattner Story and Others*; *Thirty Strange Stories*; *Certain Personal Matters*
1898	32	In poor health again; travels to Italy; meets Edmund Gosse, Henry James, Joseph Conrad, J. M. Barrie; *The War of the Worlds*
1899	33	*When the Sleeper Wakes* (in 1910 Wells revised the book and changed the title to *The Sleeper Awakes*); *Tales of Space and Time*
1900	34	Now rich enough to have house built at Sandgate, Kent; *Love and Mr Lewisham*
1901	35	*Anticipations*; *The First Men in the Moon*; birth of first son 'Gip', G. P. Wells

Year	Arts & Science	History & Politics
1892	Kipling's *Barrack Room Ballads*; Diesel's internal combustion engine	Keir Hardie wins first seat in Parliament for Labour (ILP)
1893	Henry Ford's first automobile	Gladstone's Irish Home Rule Bill defeated
1894	Shaw's *Arms and the Man*; Edison's Kinetoscope Parlour, New York; Emile Berliner's gramophone disc	Death of Alexander III, Tsar of Russia; accession of Nicholas II
1895	Conrad's *Almayer's Folly*; Freud's *Studies in Hysteria*; Wilhelm Rontgen introduces X-rays; Gillette's safety razor	Hispano-Cuban War; London School of Economics founded; Jameson Raid, South Africa
1896	Chekhov's *The Seagull*; Nobel Prizes instituted; William Ramsay discovers helium. Rutherford publishes researches into magnetic detection of electrical waves; Becquerel determines radioactivity of Uranium	Cecil Rhodes resigns as PM of Cape Colony
1897	Shaw's *Candida*; The Webbs's *Industrial Democracy*; Havelock Ellis's *Studies in the Psychology of Sex*; Robert Ross discovers the cause of malaria; Marconi's first radio transmission	Queen Victoria's Diamond Jubilee; Indian revolt on North West Frontier
1898	Zola's *J'Accuse*; Wilde's *The Ballad of Reading Gaol*; Henry James's *The Turn of the Screw*; the Curies discover radium	Cuban-American War; death of Bismarck; Battle of Omdurman, Sudan; General Kitchener retakes Khartoum
1899	Wilde's *The Importance of Being Earnest*	Dreyfus pardoned; Boer War begins
1900	Conrad's *Lord Jim*; Chekhov's *Uncle Vanya*; Freud's *The Interpretation of Dreams*; Planck's Quantum Theory; deaths of Ruskin and Wilde	Boxer Rebellion in China
1901	Kipling's *Kim*; Thomas Mann's *Buddenbrooks*; Marconi transmits radio communication across the Atlantic	Assassination of President McKinley, USA; Theodore Roosevelt succeeds; Queen Victoria dies; accession of Edward VII

Year	Age	Life
1902	36	*The Sea Lady*; *The Discovery of the Future*
1903	37	Joins Fabian Society, the Coefficients, and the Reform Club; birth of second son, Frank; *Twelve Stories and a Dream*; *Mankind in the Making*
1904	38	*The Food of the Gods*
1905	39	*Kipps*; *A Modern Utopia*
1906	40	Affairs with Amber Reeves and Rosamund Bland; meets Gorky in New York; *In the Days of the Comet*; *Socialism and the Family*; *The Future in America*; *The So-called Science of Sociology*; *Faults of the Fabian Society*; *The Reconstruction of the Fabian Society*
1907	41	*This Misery of Boots*
1908	42	Resigns from the Fabians; *First and Last Things*; *The War in the Air*; *New Worlds for Old*
1909	43	Birth of Wells's daughter, Anna, to Amber Reeves; Wells and Jane move to Hampstead; *Tono-Bungay*; *Ann Veronica*
1910	44	*The History of Mr Polly*

Year	Arts & Science	History & Politics
1902	Conrad's *Heart of Darkness*; Bennett's *Anna of the Five Towns*; William James's *The Varieties of Religious Experience*; Caruso's first record	End of the Boer War
1903	The Wright Brothers succeed in powered flight; Henry Ford starts Ford Motors; Samuel Butler's *The Way of All Flesh*; Shaw's *Man & Superman*	Bolshevik–Menshevik split in Russian socialists; Lenin becomes Bolshevik leader
1904	Picasso's *The Two Sisters*; Freud's *The Psychopathology of Everyday Life*; Chekhov's *The Cherry Orchard*	Russo-Japanese War begins; Theodore Roosevelt re-elected
1905	Einstein's Special Theory of Relativity; Débussy's *La Mer*; Cézanne's *Les Grandes; Baigneuses*; Edith Wharton's *House of Mirth*; Shaw's *Major Barbara* forbidden by New York police	Russia defeated by Japan; riots in St Petersburg, 'the Potemkin' mutinies
1906	J. J. Thompson wins Nobel Prize for Physics	American occupation of Cuba; Liberal victory in General Election – maj. 218; Labour win 54 seats
1907	First Cubist exhibition in Paris; Kipling's Nobel Prize for Literature; Conrad's *The Secret Agent*	Defeat of Labour bill to give votes to women; arrest of fifty-seven suffragettes in London
1908	Arnold Bennett's *The Old Wives' Tale*; E. M. Forster's *A Room with a View*; Rutherford wins Nobel Prize for Physics; Wright Brothers tour Europe	Asquith Prime Minister; Mrs Pankhurst imprisoned
1909	Diaghilev's Russian Ballet in Paris; Peary Expedition at North Pole; Blériot flies the Channel	Murderer Dr Crippen arrested
1910	Marie Curie's *Treatise on Radiography*; Stravinsky's *Firebird*; Roger Fry's Post-Impressionist Exhibition in London; E. M. Forster's *Howards End*; Tolstoy dies	Death of Edward VII; accession of George V

Year	Age	Life
1911	45	*The New Machiavelli*; *The Country of the Blind and Other Stories*; *Floor Games* (for children); moves to Easton Glebe, Essex
1912	46	Meets Rebecca West; *Marriage*; *The Great State*; *The Labour Unrest*
1913	47	*The Passionate Friends*; *Little Wars*; *War and Commonsense*
1914	48	Birth of Wells's son, Anthony, to Rebecca West; visits Russia with Maurice Baring; *The Wife of Sir Isaac Harman*; *The World Set Free*; *An Englishman Looks at the World*; *The War That Will End War*
1915	49	*Boon* (originally published under the pseudonym Reginald Bliss); break with Henry James; *The Research Magnificent*; *Bealby*; *The Peace of the World*
1916	50	Visits Western Front in France and Italy; *Mr Britling Sees it Through*; *The Elements of Reconstruction*; *What is Coming?*
1917	51	*The Soul of a Bishop*; *Wars and the Future*; *God, the Invisible King*; *A Reasonable Man's Peace*
1918	52	*Joan and Peter*; *In the Fourth Year*; *British Nationalism and the League of Nations*; joins Ministry of Information under Lord Northcliffe
1919	53	*The Undying Fire*; *History is One*; contributor to *The Idea of a League of Nations*; *The Way to a League of Nations*

Year	Arts & Science	History & Politics
1911	Amundsen at South Pole; Rutherford's *Theory of Atomic Structure*; D. H. Lawrence's *The White Peacock*; Ezra Pound's *Cantos*; Rupert Brooke's *Poems*	Lords Reform Bill passed in Lords after intervention of the King; Liberals announce first measures for National Insurance
1912	Schoenberg's *Pierrot Lunaire*; Jung's *The Theory of Psychoanalysis*	The *Titanic* disaster; Woodrow Wilson elected US President
1913	Vitamin A isolated at Yale, by Elmer McCollum; Lawrence's *Sons and Lovers*	Panama Canal opened; hunger strikes by Suffragettes in prison
1914	J. H. Jean's *Radiation and the Quantum Theory*; James Joyce's *Dubliners*	Assassination of Archduke Franz Ferdinand of Austria in Sarajevo; the Great War starts
1915	D. W. Griffith's film *Birth of a Nation*; Somerset Maugham's *Of Human Bondage*; Lawrence's *The Rainbow* banned; Joseph Conrad's *Victory*	The Allied failure at Gallipoli; Zeppelins attack London; The *Lusitania* sinking; Coalition Government formed in Britain
1916	Death of Henry James; Joyce's *Portrait of the Artist as a Young Man*; Dadaism in Zurich	The battle of Verdun; the Easter Rising, Dublin; Battle of Jutland; President Wilson's plea for peace; Lloyd George Prime Minister
1917	Freud's *Introduction to Psychoanalysis*; T. S. Eliot's *Prufrock*	America enters the war; Russian Revolution; Lenin in power; Woodrow Wilson re-elected
1918	Matisse's *Odalisques*; Joyce's *Ulysses*	Collapse of the Central Powers ends the Great War; Versailles Peace Conference; vote given to women over thirty and men over twenty-one; first woman elected to Parliament – Countess Markiewicz (Sinn Fein)
1919	Thomas H. Morgan's *The Physical Basis of Heredity*; Thomas Hardy's *Collected Poems*; Maugham's *The Moon and Sixpence*; J. M. Keynes's *The Economic Consequences of the Peace*; Bauhaus founded; Alcock and Brown fly the Atlantic	Herbert Hoover takes control of European Relief; Prohibition in America; Versailles Treaty signed; President Wilson awarded Nobel Peace Prize; socialist uprising in Berlin crushed by troops; murder of Rosa Luxembourg

Year	Age	Life
1920	54	Visits Russia ; meets Lenin and Moura Budberg ; *The Outline of History* ; *Russia in the Shadows*
1921	55	Visits USA ; *The Salvaging of Civilization* ; *The New Teaching of History*
1922	56	*A Short History of the World* ; *The Secret Places of the Heart* ; *University of London Address* ; unsuccessful as a Labour Parliamentary candidate for London University
1923	57	*Men Like Gods* ; *The Story of a Great Schoolmaster* ; *To the Electors of London University* ; *The Labour Ideal of Education* ; stands for Parliament again but defeated
1924	58	Begins affair with Odette Keun ; *The Dream* ; *The P. R. Parliament*
1925	59	*Christina Alberta's Father* ; *A Forecast of World Affairs*
1926	60	*The World of William Clissold* ; *Mr Belloc Objects*
1927	61	Death of Jane Wells ; *Meanwhile* ; *Collected Short Stories* ; *Democracy Under Revision* ; collected H. G. Wells (Atlantic edition) completed in USA
1928	62	*The Open Conspiracy: Blue Prints for a World Revolution* ; *Mr Blettsworthy on Rampole Island* ; introduction to *The Book of Catherine Wells* ; *The Way the World is Going*

Year	Arts & Science	History & Politics
1920	Eddington's *Space, Time and Gravitation*; F. Scott Fitzgerald's *This Side of Paradise*; Sinclair Lewis's *Main Street*; Edith Wharton's *The Age of Innocence*	America rejects the League of Nations; National Socialist Workers party (NAZI) publishes manifesto, Germany
1921	Einstein wins Nobel Prize for Physics	Victory of Red Army in Russian Civil War
1922	T. S. Eliot's *The Waste Land*; first transmissions by BBC	Mussolini establishes dictatorship in Italy; Irish Free State established
1923	Gershwin's *Rhapsody in Blue*; E. N. da C. Andrade's *The Structure of the Atom*; Freud's *The Ego and the Id*; W. B. Yeats awarded Nobel Prize for Literature	Hitler's NAZI coup fails in Munich; Stanley Baldwin Prime Minister; Matrimonial Bill passed, allowing wives to divorce husbands; British Mandate in Palestine
1924	E. M. Forster's *A Passage to India*; Thomas Mann's *Magic Mountain*	Lenin dies; Minority Labour government; Ramsay MacDonald Prime Minister
1925	John Logie Baird's successful television experiments; Eisenstein's film *Battleship Potemkin*; Chaplin's *The Gold Rush*; Fitzgerald's *The Great Gatsby*	Hitler publishes *Mein Kampf*
1926	Fritz Lang's film *Metropolis*; William Faulkner's *Soldier's Pay*; Kafka's *The Castle*; Hemingway's *The Sun also Rises*; R. H. Tawney's *Religion and the Rise of Capitalism*	British troops withdraw from the Rhineland; British Commonwealth instituted; General Strike
1927	Lindbergh's flight from New York to Paris; Abel Gance's film *Napoleon*; Virginia Woolf's *To the Lighthouse*; *The Jazz Singer* (first talkie); completion of Proust's *A la Recherche du Temps Perdu*	Trotsky expelled from Russian Communist Party
1928	J. L. Baird demonstrates colour TV; Eisenstein's film *October*	Vote given to women over twenty-one – equal rights; Chiang Kai-shek President of China

Year	Age	Life
1929	63	First broadcasts on BBC ; *The Adventures of Tommy* (for children) ; film script of *The King Who Was a King* ; *Imperialism and the Open Conspiracy*
1930	64	Moves back to London ; *The Autocracy of Mr Parham*
1931	65	*The Science of Life* (A Summary of Contemporary Knowledge about Life and its Possibilities with Julian Huxley and G. P. Wells) ; diagnosed as diabetic ; *What Are We To Do With Our Lives ?* ; *The Queer Story of Brownlow's Newspaper* ; *The Way to World Peace*
1932	66	*The Bulpington of Bulp* ; *The Work, Wealth and Happiness of Mankind* ; *After Democracy*
1933	67	Begins affair with Moura Budberg ; *The Shape of Things to Come*
1934	68	Talks with Stalin and with F. D. Roosevelt ; *Experiment in Autobiography*
1935	69	Works with Alexander Korda on film version of *The Shape of Things to Come* ; *The New America*

Year	Arts & Science	History & Politics
1929	Robert Graves's *Goodbye to All That*; Hemingway's *A Farewell to Arms*; Thomas Mann wins Nobel Prize for Literature	Crash of New York Stock Exchange, Wall Street; Second Minority Labour Government; thirteen women elected to Parliament; NAZI victory in Bavarian elections
1930	Freud's *Civilization and its Discontents*; W. H. Auden's *Poems*; Robert Frost's *Collected Poems*; Sinclair Lewis wins Nobel Prize for Literature; Amy Johnson's flight from London to Australia; death of D. H. Lawrence	Haile Selassie (Ras Tafari) becomes Emperor of Ethiopia; Gandhi's Salt March, India; NAZI party becomes second largest in Germany
1931	Death of Edison; Empire State Building completed; Chaplin's *City Lights*; Schweitzer's *My Life and Thoughts*; Faulkner's *Sanctuary*	World slump begins with the collapse of the Credit Anstadt bank, Vienna; first woman elected to the American Senate; National Government, Britain
1932	James Chadwick discovers the neutron; Fritz Lang's film of Huxley's *Brave New World*; Galsworthy's Nobel Prize for Literature	Franklin D. Roosevelt wins US Presidential election; New Deal initiated; Stalin purges begin, Russia
1933	A. N. Whitehead's *Adventures of Ideas*; Jung's *Psychology and Religion*; Orwell's *Down and Out in Paris and London*	Hitler becomes Chancellor; start of anti-Jewish measures in Germany; first concentration camps; Germany leaves League of Nations
1934	Gershwin's *Porgy and Bess*; Graves's *I Claudius*	'Night of the Long Knives' massacre in Germany; Hitler assumes title of 'Führer', after plebiscite
1935	The Curies awarded Nobel Prize for Chemistry, having synthesized radioactive elements; The Webbs's *Soviet Communism; A New Civilization*; Graham Greene's *England Made Me*; T. S. Eliot's *Murder in the Cathedral*	Hitler denounces Versailles Treaty, forms Air Force and imposes conscription; Russian Show Trials; Italy invades Abyssinia

Year   Age Life

1936   70   Awarded Hon.D.Litt by London University; *The Anatomy of Frustration*; *The Croquet Player*; *The Idea of a World Encyclopaedia*

1937   71   *Brynhild*; *Star Begotten*; *The Camford Visitation*; *The Informative Content of Education*; (film) *The Man Who Could Work Miracles*

1938   72   *Apropos of Dolores*; *World Brain*; *The Brothers*

1939   73   Visits Sweden; *The Fate Of Homo Sapiens*; *Travels of a Republican Radical In Search of Hot Water*; *The Holy Terror*

1940   74   In London during Blitz; speaking tour of USA; *The Commonsense of War and Peace* (originally given as address to German Reichstag in 1929); *Babes in the Darkling Wood*; *All Aboard for Ararat*

1941   75   *Guide to the New World*; *You Can't be Too Careful*

1942   76   *Phoenix*; *Science and the World Mind*; The Conquest of Time (final revision of *First and Last Things*); *The Outlook for Homo Sapiens*

1943   77   *Crux Ansata*

Year	Arts & Science	History & Politics
1936	Chaplin's *Modern Times*; Alexander Korda's film *Things to Come*; Dylan Thomas's *Twenty-five Poems*; Kipling Houseman and Chesterton die; A. J. Ayer's *Language, Truth and Logic*	Hitler reoccupies the Rhineland; Spanish Civil War begins; Rome–Berlin Axis announced; death of George V; Edward VIII accedes in January, abdicates in December; 'Battle of Cable St' in London's East End
1937	Picasso's *Guernica*; Steinbeck's *Of Mice and Men*; Orwell's *The Road to Wigan Pier*; Sartre's *La Nausée*; Wallace Carothers invents nylon	Stalin purges high Party and military officials; Japanese Imperialism in China, Peking and Shanghai captured
1938	Orson Welles's radio feature of H. G. Wells's *The War of the Worlds* terrifies America	Austria falls to Hitler; Munich Conference over Czechoslovakia; Appeasement Policy confirmed; Franco's victories in Spain; Roosevelt appeals to the dictators for peace
1939	Death of Freud; Jolie-Curie shows the potential of nuclear fission. Henry Moore's *Reclining Figure*; Joyce's *Finnegan's Wake*; Steinbeck's *The Grapes of Wrath*; death of Yeats, and of Ford Madox Ford	Germany invades Poland; Second World War begins; Hitler–Stalin Pact; Russia invades Finland and Poland; fall of Madrid to Franco
1940	Koestler's *Darkness at Noon*	Churchill Prime Minister; Dunkirk and collapse of France; Battle of Britain; start of Blitz on London; murder of Trotsky
1941	Welles's *Citizen Kane*; Carrol Reed's film *Kipps*	Hitler invades Russia; Japan bombs Pearl Harbor; America enters the War
1942	Evelyn Waugh's *Put Out More Flags*	Japan invades Burma, Malaya, Dutch East Indies; Singapore surrenders; Americans bomb Tokyo; Stalingrad siege begins; Montgomery wins El Alamein; start of Hitler's 'Final Solution'
1943	Henry Moore's sculpture *Madonna and Child*	Russian victory at Stalingrad; Warsaw Ghetto killings; Allies finally conquer North Africa; fall of Mussolini, Italy surrenders

Year	Age	Life
1944	78	'42 to '44 : A Contemporary Memoir ; thesis for Doctorate of Science (On the Quality of Illusion in the Continuity of the Individual Life in the Higher Metazoa with Particular Reference to the Species Homo Sapiens) ; in London during rocket attacks
1945	79	Mind at the End of Its Tether ; The Happy Turning ; The Betterave Papers
1946		Dies in London, 13 August

Year	Arts & Science	History & Politics
1944	T. S. Eliot's *Four Quartets*	Leningrad relieved; Allies capture Rome and land in Normandy; de Gaulle enters Paris; V1 and V2 rocket raids on London
1945	Orwell's *Animal Farm*; Nobel Prize for medicine to Alexander Fleming, E. B. Chain and Howard Florey, for discovery of penicillin	Yalta Conference; Russians capture Warsaw and Berlin; Mussolini executed, Hitler's suicide; United Nations Charter; end of the Second World War in Europe; death of President Roosevelt; atomic bombs dropped on Hiroshima and Nagasaki; Japan surrenders; Labour win General Election; Attlee Prime Minister
1946	Electronic Brain constructed at Pennsylvania University; Cocteau's film *La Belle et La Bête*; Eugene O'Neill's *The Iceman Cometh*	First General Assembly of the United Nations; nationalization of Civil Aviation, coal and the Bank of England; Churchill's 'Iron Curtain' speech
1947	Transistor invented	GATT established
1948	Norman Mailer's *The Naked and the Dead*	National Health Service; Israel founded; East German blockade of Berlin; Allied airlift into Berlin
1949	Orwell's *1984*	West Germany established, confirming division of Europe
1950	Death of Orwell	Start of Korean War

INTRODUCTION

On that special bookshelf reserved for tales of people ship-wrecked on desert islands, none is more sinister and compelling than H. G. Wells's *The Island of Doctor Moreau*. It competes in abiding interest with other durables on that shelf, Daniel Defoe's *Robinson Crusoe*, Swift's *Gulliver's Travels*, and William Golding's *The Lord of the Flies*. Much like its neighbours, *Moreau* is a morality play. Jorge Luis Borges called it 'an atrocious miracle'.

In the course of a long and controversial career, Herbert George Wells (1866–1946) published over one hundred books. *Doctor Moreau* comes very early in the canon. It was published by William Heinemann in 1896, when Wells was thirty years old and in ill health. His wonderful short novel, *The Time Machine*, had appeared in the previous year, and his collection of short stories, *The Stolen Bacillus*. *The Invisible Man* was to follow in the succeeding year, with the novel that would secure his name, *The War of the Worlds*, in 1898.

Doctor Moreau was unfavourably received by the critics, as satirical and fantastic novels frequently are. When *Gulliver's Travels* was first published, Swift wrote with glee to Alexander Pope to say that a learned Irish bishop had been overheard remarking that 'he didn't believe a word of it'. These days, we are more accustomed to horror stories in real life than perhaps were the late Victorians; *Doctor Moreau* has achieved perfect credibility in the days of 'ethnic cleansing'.

Whereas *Robinson Crusoe* tells the story of a solitary man who comes to terms with his solitude through his own resourcefulness and his relationship with God (though other interpretations of Defoe's novel are on offer), *Doctor Moreau* is the story of a crowd of beings whose god is the source of all their miseries.

The similarities between Defoe and Wells have seldom been noted. Living almost two centuries apart, both men were the sort of prolific English writer who produces a stream of pamphlets and treatises as well as novels. Both became involved in politics, Wells on a high level. Defoe's great novel exerts an influence on almost any writer who has read him, including Wells. Yet Wells's story is about as original as a story may be without becoming ridiculous, for all the literary tradition behind it. Wells's brilliant conclusion certainly carries a strong flavour of Swift's bitter herb at the end of Gulliver's voyage to the Country of the Houyhnhnms. *Doctor Moreau* comes from the prolific and inspired decade in Wells's career, when he was a great assimilator of influences as well as an originator.

And why did he enjoy Swift? One reason is because Swift in some measure seems to give early utterance to those evolutionary themes which Wells pursues in all his scientific romances.

Wells was involved in the great religious–scientific debate which encompassed many of the finest minds of the nineteenth century – a debate still to be concluded. He stood, as it were, as the Candidate for Rationality, that rationality by means of which mankind would divest itself. The time was coming, Wells prophesied, when mankind would break forth from its dirty cities, its pathetic limitations of mentality, its ill condition, to become splendid and to establish Utopia here on Earth – and doubtless elsewhere in the universe. He was the first man to develop a programme for the future of the race and broadcast it in popular terms. Wells longed for – and more importantly worked for – the time when there would be – to appropriate one of his titles – *Men Like Gods*.

This optimistic side to Wells's character was in conflict with a darker aspect: what Jung calls the Shadow side. His generation believed, perhaps more fervently than we are able to do, in the disinterested power of knowledge to improve life; but Wells was not unaware of how easy it was to abuse knowledge. His novel, *The Invisible Man*, is a tale of knowledge misused. So, too, is *Doctor Moreau* – and also somewhat more complex than such an easy phrase may suggest.

A new kind of knowledge was on the table in Wells's day. He followed his great teacher, Thomas Huxley, in his devotion to the fresh truths and insights which evolution was bringing to human understanding. Nowhere do we see more clearly than in Wells's books the workings of a revolution in thought which troubled the second half of Victoria's reign and continues to haunt our century. Evolution seemed to bring a terrible light to bear on everyday affairs, not least upon moralities, and not least because it ranked mankind as only quantitatively, not qualitatively, different from the animal kingdom, thus discountenancing the Christian God of previous generations, if not banishing him entirely. We were up from the Ape, not down from the Angels. We carried in our anatomies proof of the ancestral beast.

This new and enlightened view held immense attraction for Wells, and not only for the acuity of the Darwinian argument informing it. It appealed also to his darker side. Humankind was no great distance from the brutes – as he himself had yet to put distance between himself and his working class origins, with the primitive living conditions described in many of his novels. The education of the poor beasts on Moreau's island, by rote and whip, was not a million miles distant from the 'crammers' to which Wells himself had been subjected.

So Wells pitches his dark fable right in the middle of his own struggles as well as the philosophical struggles of his day. Moreau's island stands as a model for the world and Moreau himself as a model for God the cruel experimental Scientist.

Wells is precise about this, referring to his novel as 'a youthful exercise in blasphemy'. Moreau is depicted as 'a white-faced white-haired man, with calm eyes. Save for his serenity, the touch almost of beauty that resulted from his set tranquillity and from his magnificent build, he might have passed muster among a hundred other comfortable old gentlemen.' It is a description of the Old Testament God, as depicted in the illustrations of a million Victorian Bibles.

In the grim world over which Moreau presides, human beings are presented as little more than animals. And those animals are tortured by the cruel randomness of natural selection. 'It's a chance, I tell you,' says Montgomery, early on. 'As everything is in a man's life.'

A reader need care little for the scientific background to enjoy the story superficially, as a swift-moving and terrifying tale. But there are concealed elements to *Doctor Moreau* which deepen our appreciation of it.

Like Mary Shelley's *Frankenstein, Doctor Moreau* tells of the making of human beings by other than natural means.

Doctor Moreau is another irresponsible scientist in the manner of Victor Frankenstein. And, as in *Frankenstein*, the story opens with a sea voyage.

The protagonist, Edward Prendick, arrives at Moreau's island only after a shipwreck. As if to prove Montgomery's point, it is by chance that the 'Mary Vain' collides with a derelict and sinks. Prendick has to take his chance in a dinghy with two other men. They draw lots to see which shall survive. By luck, Prendick is picked up by a schooner. 'Chance, just chance,' says his rescuer: not the well-known Hand of God. Natural selection has chosen Prendick.

The drunken captain of the schooner is no less a model for the merciless Moreau to come (just as Captain Walton in *Frankenstein* is a model for Victor Frankenstein, the man he picks up off the ice floe). The captain says, 'I am the law here – the law and the prophets', thus giving us a kind of parodic prologue to the main action; here is another petty substitute for God, crudely ruling the world of his ship.

Moreau rules everything on his island. He has the unreliable Montgomery under him. Prendick constitutes the third human. Besides this trio there are only the Beast People, 'human in shape, yet human beings with the strangest air about them of some familiar animal'. Gradually, we are taken deeper into the mysteries of nature – or what distortions pass for nature on this island.

It is very much part of Wells's intention that Prendick is soon being hunted like an animal, and hides like an animal in the scrub of the island: the boundary lines between men and animals are continually blurred. Is it human, is it beast? Prendick, in an agony of fear, comes to the wrong conclusion, and has to be pursued, hunted down, by Moreau before he understands the truth of what is happening on the island.

Moreau has his reasons. He *is* reason. He rules by his remorseless logic. 'To this day I have never troubled about the ethics of the matter. The study of Nature makes a man at last as remorseless as nature.'

This God proceeds to explain how he has slowly transformed animals into semblances of humans, not without mistakes – evolutionary errors, one might say – which perished miserably on the way. The gorilla is one such mistake, although Moreau taught it a rudimentary sense of shame.

As Moreau explains, he has little problem now with moulding a human shape. The difficulty is with the brain. At this juncture, Wells seems almost to be speaking directly about humanity rather than the animal kingdom. Moreau says, 'The intelligence is often oddly low, with unaccountable blank ends, unexpected gaps. And least satisfactory of all is something which I cannot touch, somewhere – I cannot determine where – in the seat of the emotions. Cravings, instincts, desires that harm humanity, a strange hidden reservoir to burst suddenly and inundate the whole being of the creature with anger, hate, or fear.'

No doubt Wells, like a good storyteller, was here intent on freezing the reader's blood, or at least inducing a state of mental unease (Does he mean me? is a question we often ask when reading Wells); and *Doctor Moreau* remains a frightening novel. But it must slightly have strained credulity in the 1890s to imagine that Doctor Moreau achieved what he did in the way of malign transformation purely with the scalpel. The man is no more than a vivisectionist.

The story has become even more topical these days, and certainly no less prone to freeze the blood, because we can take vivisection as a symbol for various scientific procedures available today which are much more effective and radical to their effect upon human or animal flesh: working not merely superficially but at genetic level. Our powers are infinitely greater than Moreau's; the power to create new animals which will best suit human purposes is already within our grasp. The spirit of

Doctor Moreau is alive and well and living in the late twentieth century. These days, Moreau would be state-funded.

The didacticism of the novel is well-concealed under the sleight-of-hand of an expert storyteller. As so often in Wells, the dénouement, or the sound reasoning which will make the dénouement undeniable as well as astonishing, is glimpsed early in the story. While Moreau makes his dreadful explanation to Prendick, he complains, much as a medieval theologian might imagine God to complain, 'The stubborn beast flesh grows, day by day, back again . . .'

Just as the most memorable scene in *Robinson Crusoe* is Crusoe's discovery of the alien footstep on the beach, the memorable thing in *Doctor Moreau* is the Beast People: those lumbering, slinking parodies of humanity. Wells makes them frightening, dark, depraved, and also pathetic. We grieve for them. Our conscience is involved. The Hyena-Swine, the Dog Man, the Satyr, the Wolf Woman, stay with us.

What divides the Beast People from the animal is less their near-human shape, more their ability to use language. It is in the terrible days of decline, when the beast flesh grows back again, that language slips away from them, reverting to snarls and grunts. 'Language, once clear-cut and exact [starts] softening and guttering, losing shape and import, becoming mere lumps of sound again.'

'With speech humanity begins', Wells was to say, a few years after writing *Doctor Moreau*. With the coming of speech, a boundary was crossed. He speaks of a child acquiring this wonderful instrument marking it off from the animal, likening it to a keyboard with 'thirty, forty, or fifty thousand keys', and then plunges into one of his marvellous images as he outlines what the child may achieve.

'There will come a time when, at the merest touch upon those keys, image will follow image and emotion develop into emotion, when the whole creation, the deeps of space, the minutest beauties of the microscope, cities, armies, passions, splendours, sorrows, will leap out of darkness into the conscious being of thought, when this interwoven net of brief, small sounds will form the centre of a web that will hold together in its threads the universe, the All, visible and invisible, material and immaterial, real and imagined, of a human mind.'

This comes from a book entitled, significantly, *The Making of Mankind* (1903). Mankind is expressly what the Beast People are not made into by the scalpel, by the fear of Doctor Moreau's House of Pain. They are never able to catch a glimpse of the All. What they are capable of is chanting a litany, a litany that in some aspects at least recalls a psalm that might be sung mindlessly in a Christian church: 'His is the lightning-flash: His is the deep salt sea: His are the stars in the sky.' The emphasis is on the *His*: none of these things belongs in any way to the Beast People. They are exiled from animal and human happiness alike. 'Born under one law, to another bound . . .'

Doctor Moreau is much more than 'an exercise in youthful blasphemy'. What maintains its interest for us today is that it attacks human pride, much as *The War of the Worlds* does – the idea that evolution has somehow worked especially for our benefit and that we are, in the old phrase current in Victorian times, Lords of Creation. It is this attack on faulty reasoning, and on smugness in general – rather than simply on the smugness of the Church – which keeps the fizz in the Wells bottle.

As Wells said, this short sharp shock of a novel ran counter to the placid assumption that Evolution was a pro-human force making things better and better for mankind. And he added that 'now and then the universe projects itself towards me in a hideous grimace'. It was his Shadow side speaking. Many later science fiction writers, following however unconsciously in Wells's footsteps, have been aware of that same contradiction at the heart of things.

Wells's ideas, his many ideas, of utopia involved gardens. Often those gardens contained large tame members of the cat family, weaned of their carnivorous habits. These pussies clearly have sexual significance: the linkage between them and freedom is no coincidence. Such cats appear in Wells's poignant short story, 'The Door in the Wall', and in such novels as *Men Like Gods*, *The Shape of Things to Come*, and *The Research Magnificent*. One of the great loves of Wells's active love-life was the novelist

Rebecca West; she was 'Panther' to him; he was 'Jaguar' to her. They could escape into an animal world.

A telling passage in *Doctor Moreau* – quoted to indicate something of the strange poetic inversions running through the book – comes when Prendick tracks down the escaped Leopard Man. He finds it 'crouched in the smallest possible compass', regarding Prendick over its shoulder.

> It may seem a strange contradiction in me – I cannot explain the fact – but now, seeing the creature there in a perfectly animal attitude, with the light gleaming in its eyes, and its imperfectly human face distorted with terror, I realised again the fact of its humanity. In another moment, others of its pursuers would see it, and it would be overpowered and captured, to experience once more the horrible tortures of the enclosure. Abruptly, I slipped out my revolver, aimed between his terror-struck eyes, and fired.

The ending of the novel, with its echoes of Swift's *Gulliver's Travels*, is a triumph of construction. Just as the Beast People show the failings of animals, so the humans show human weaknesses. Moreau dies and is assumed to be in heaven, Montgomery takes to drink, Prendick is unable to assert authority. And the Beast People – inevitably they revert to something even more vile than the Beast which was never eradicated within them.

There are many final ironies, which readers must relish on their own account. Dark though the vision of *Doctor Moreau* is, it carries an inner light, since it is addressed to us, the readers, in the conviction that we will understand and that we too, conscious of 'the universe, the All', will appreciate it not only as a splendid example of storytelling but as one of those cautions we can apply to ourselves, warding off the ever-incipient Beast-flesh.

BRIAN ALDISS

'I could not distinguish what he said.'
(Frontispiece to first edition of 1896 by C. R. Ashbee)

THE ISLAND OF
DOCTOR MOREAU

Introduction

On February the 1st, 1887, the *Lady Vain* was lost by collision with a derelict when about the latitude 1° s. and longitude 107° w.

On January the 5th, 1888 – that is, eleven months and four days after – my uncle, Edward Prendick, a private gentleman, who certainly went aboard the *Lady Vain* at Callao, and who had been considered drowned, was picked up in latitude 5° 3′ s. and longitude 101° w. in a small open boat, of which the name was illegible, but which is supposed to have belonged to the missing schooner *Ipecacuanha*. He gave such a strange account of himself that he was supposed demented. Subsequently, he alleged that his mind was a blank from the moment of his escape from the *Lady Vain*. His case was discussed among psychologists at the time as a curious instance of the lapse of memory consequent upon physical and mental stress. The following narrative was found among his papers by the undersigned, his nephew and heir, but unaccompanied by any definite request for publication.

The only island known to exist in the region in which my uncle was picked up is Noble's Isle, a small volcanic islet, and uninhabited. It was visited in 1891 by HMS *Scorpion*. A party of sailors then landed, but found nothing living thereon except certain curious white moths, some hogs and rabbits, and some rather peculiar rats. No specimen was secured of these. So that this narrative is without confirmation in its most essential particular. With that understood, there seems no harm in putting this strange story before the public, in accordance, as I believe, with my uncle's intentions. There is at least this much in its behalf: my uncle passed out of human knowledge about latitude 5° s. and longitude 105° E., and reappeared in the same part of the ocean after a space of eleven months. In some way he must have lived during the interval. And it seems that a schooner called the *Ipecacuanha*, with a drunken captain, John Davis, did start from Africa with a puma and certain other animals aboard in January 1887, that the vessel was well known at several ports in the South Pacific, and that it finally disappeared from those seas (with a considerable amount of copra aboard), sailing to its unknown fate from Banya in December 1887, a date that tallies entirely with my uncle's story.

Charles Edward Prendick

I
In the Dingey of the 'Lady Vain'

I do not propose to add anything to what has already been written concerning the loss of the *Lady Vain*. As every one knows, she collided with a derelict when ten days out from Callao. The long-boat with seven of the crew was picked up eighteen days after by HM gunboat *Myrtle*, and the story of their privations has become almost as well known as the far more terrible *Medusa* case. I have now, however, to add to the published story of the *Lady Vain* another as horrible, and certainly far stranger. It has hitherto been supposed that the four men who were in the dingey perished, but this is incorrect. I have the best of evidence for this assertion – I am one of the four men.

But, in the first place, I must state that there never were four men in the dingey; the number was three. Constans, who was 'seen by the captain to jump into the gig' (*Daily News*, March 17, 1887), luckily for us, and unluckily for himself, did not reach us. He came down out of the tangle of ropes under the stays of the smashed bowsprit; some small rope caught his heel as he let go, and he hung for a moment head downward, and then fell and struck a block or spar floating in the water. We pulled towards him, but he never came up.

I say, luckily for us he did not reach us, and I might almost add luckily for himself, for there were only a small breaker of water and some soddened ship's biscuits with us – so sudden had been the alarm, so unprepared the ship for any disaster. We thought the people on the launch would be better provisioned (though it seems they were not), and we tried to hail them. They could not have heard us, and the next morning when the drizzle cleared – which was not until past mid-day – we could see nothing of them. We could not stand up to look about us because of the pitching of the boat. The sea ran in great rollers, and we had much ado to keep the boat's head to them. The two other men who had escaped so far with me were a man named Helmar, a passenger like myself, and a seaman whose name I don't know, a short sturdy man with a stammer.

We drifted famishing, and, after our water had come to an end, tormented by an intolerable thirst, for eight days altogether. After the second day the sea subsided slowly to a glassy calm. It is quite impossible for the ordinary reader to imagine those eight days. He has not – luckily for himself – anything in his memory to imagine with. After the first day we said little to one another, and lay in our places in the boat and stared at the horizon, or watched, with eyes that grew larger and more haggard every day, the misery and weakness gaining upon our companions. The sun became pitiless. The water ended on the fourth day, and we were already thinking strange things and saying them with our eyes; but it was, I think, the sixth before Helmar gave voice to the thing we all had in mind. I remember our voices dry and thin, so that we bent towards one another and spared our words. I stood out against it with all my might, was rather for scuttling the boat and perishing together among the sharks that followed us; but when Helmar said that if his proposal was accepted we should have drink, the sailor came round to him.

I would not draw lots, however, and in the night the sailor whispered to Helmar again and again, and I sat in the bows with my clasp-knife in my hand – though I doubt if I had the stuff in me to fight. And in the morning I agreed to Helmar's proposal and we handed halfpence to find the odd man.

The lot fell upon the sailor, but he was the strongest of us and would not abide by it, and attacked Helmar with his hands. They grappled together and almost stood up. I crawled along the boat to them, intending to help Helmar by grasping the sailor's leg, but the sailor stumbled with the swaying of the boat, and the two fell upon the gunwale and rolled overboard together. They sank like stones. I remember laughing at that and wondering why I laughed. The laugh caught me suddenly like a thing from without.

I lay across one of the thwarts for I know not how long,

thinking that if I had the strength I would drink sea-water and madden myself to die quickly. And even as I lay there, I saw, with no more interest than if it had been a picture, a sail come up towards me over the sky-line. My mind must have been wandering, and yet I remember all that happened quite distinctly. I remember how my head swayed with the seas, and the horizon with the sail above it danced up and down. But I also remember as distinctly that I had a persuasion that I was dead, and that I thought what a jest it was they should come too late by such a little to catch me in my body.

For an endless period, as it seemed to me, I lay with my head on the thwart watching the dancing schooner – she was a little ship, schooner-rigged fore and aft – come up out of the sea. She kept tacking to and fro in a widening compass, for she was sailing dead into the wind. It never entered my head to attempt to attract attention, and I do not remember anything distinctly after the sight of her side, until I found myself in a little cabin aft. There's a dim half-memory of being lifted up to the gangway and of a big red countenance, covered with freckles and surrounded with red hair, staring at me over the bulwarks. I also had a disconnected impression of a dark face with extraordinary eyes close to mine, but that I thought was a nightmare, until I met it again. I fancy I recollect some stuff being poured in between my teeth. And that is all.

2

The Man who was Going Nowhere

The cabin in which I found myself was small, and rather untidy. A youngish man with flaxen hair, a bristly straw-coloured moustache, and a dropping nether lip was sitting and holding my wrist. For a minute we stared at one another without speaking. He had watery grey eyes, oddly void of expression.

Then just overhead came a sound like an iron bedstead being knocked about and the low angry growling of some large animal. At the same time the man spoke again.

He repeated the question : 'How do you feel now ?'

I think I said I felt all right. I could not recollect how I had got there. He must have seen the question in my face, for my voice was inaccessible to me.

'You were picked up in a boat – starving. The name on the boat was the *Lady Vain*, and there were spots of blood on the gunwale.' At the same time my eye caught my hand, so thin that it looked like a dirty skin purse full of loose bones, and all the business of the boat came back to me.

'Have some of this,' said he, and gave me a dose of some scarlet stuff, iced.

It tasted like blood, and made me feel stronger.

'You were in luck,' said he, 'to get picked up by a ship with a medical man aboard.' He spoke with a slobbering articulation, with the ghost of a lisp.

'What ship is this ?' I said slowly, hoarse from my long silence.

'It's a little trader from Arica and Callao. I never asked where she came from in the beginning. Out of the land of born fools, I guess. I'm a passenger myself from Arica. The silly ass who owns her – he's captain too, named Davis – he's lost his certificate or something. You know the kind of man – calls the thing the *Ipecacuanha* – of all silly infernal names, though when there's much of a sea without any wind she certainly acts accordingly.'

Then the noise overhead began a gain, a snarling growl and the voice of a human being together. Then another voice telling some 'Heaven-forsaken idiot' to desist.

'You were nearly dead,' said my interlocutor. 'It was a very near thing indeed. But I've put some stuff into you now. Notice your arm's sore? Injections. You've been insensible for nearly thirty hours.'

I thought slowly. I was distracted now by the yelping of a number of dogs. 'Am I eligible for solid food?' I asked.

'Thanks to me,' he said. 'Even now the mutton is boiling.'

'Yes,' I said, with assurance; 'I could eat some mutton.'

'But,' said he, with a momentary hesitation, 'you know I'm dying to hear of how you came to be alone in the boat.' I thought I detected a certain suspicion in his eyes.

'*Damn that howling!*'

He suddenly left the cabin, and I heard him in violent controversy with some one, who seemed to me to talk gibberish in response to him. The matter sounded as though it ended in blows, but in that I thought my ears were mistaken. Then he shouted at the dogs and returned to the cabin.

'Well?' said he, in the doorway. 'You were just beginning to tell me.'

I told him my name, Edward Prendick, and how I had taken to natural history as a relief from the dulness of my comfortable independence. He seemed interested in this. 'I've done some science myself – I did my Biology at University College, – getting out the ovary of the earthworm and the radula of the snail and all that. Lord! it's ten years ago. But go on, go on – tell me about the boat.'

He was evidently satisfied with the frankness of my story, which I told in concise sentences enough – for I felt horribly weak, – and when it was finished he reverted at once to the topic of natural history and his own biological studies. He began to question me closely about Tottenham Court Road and Gower Street. 'Is Caplatzi still flourishing? What a shop that was!' He had evidently been a very ordinary medical student, and drifted incontinently to the topic of the music-halls. He told me some anecdotes. 'Left it all,' he said, 'ten years ago. How jolly it all used to be ! But I made a young ass of myself . . . Played myself out before I was twenty-one. I daresay it's all different now . . . But I must look up that ass of a cook and see what he's doing to your mutton.'

The growling overhead was renewed, so suddenly and with so much savage anger that it startled me. 'What's that ?' I called after him, but the door had closed. He came back again with the boiled mutton, and I was so excited by the appetising smell of it, that I forgot the noise of the beast forthwith.

After a day of alternate sleep and feeding I was so far recovered as to be able to get from my bunk to the scuttle and see the green seas trying to keep pace with us. I judged the schooner was running before the wind. Montgomery – that was the name of the flaxen-haired man – came in again as I stood there, and I asked him for some clothes. He lent me some duck things of his own, for those I had worn in the boat, he said, had been thrown overboard. They were rather loose for me, for he was large, and long in the limbs.

He told me casually that the captain was three-parts drunk in his own cabin. As I assumed the clothes I began asking him some questions about the destination of the ship. He said the ship was bound to Hawaii, but that it had to land him first.

'Where ?' said I.

'It's an island . . . Where I live. So far as I know, it hasn't got a name.'

He stared at me with his nether lip dropping, and looked so wilfully stupid of a sudden that it came into my head that he desired to avoid my questions. I had the discretion to ask no more.

3
The Strange Face

We left the cabin and found a man at the companion obstructing our way. He was standing on the ladder with his back to us, peering over the combing of the hatchway. He was, I could see, a mis-shapen man, short, broad, and clumsy, with a crooked back, a hairy neck, and a head sunk between his shoulders. He was dressed in dark blue serge, and had peculiarly thick coarse black hair. I heard the unseen dogs growl furiously, and forthwith he ducked back, coming into contact with the hand I put out to fend him off from myself. He turned with animal swiftness.

In some indefinable way the black face thus flashed upon me shocked me profoundly. It was a singularly deformed one. The facial part projected, forming something dimly suggestive of a muzzle, and the huge half-open mouth showed as big white teeth as I had ever seen in a human mouth. His eyes were bloodshot at the edges, with scarcely a rim of white round the hazel pupils. There was a curious glow of excitement in his face.

'Confound you !' said Montgomery. 'Why the devil don't you get out of the way ?' The black-faced man started aside without a word.

I went on up the companion, instinctively staring at him as I did so. Montgomery stayed at the foot for a moment. 'You have no business here, you know,' he said, in a deliberate tone. 'Your place is forward.'

The black-faced man cowered. 'They . . . won't have me forward.' He spoke slowly, with a queer hoarse quality in his voice.

'Won't have you forward !' said Montgomery in a menacing tone. 'But I tell you to go.' He was on the brink of saying something further, then looked up at me suddenly and followed me up the ladder. I had paused halfway through the hatchway, looking back, still astonished beyond measure at the grotesque ugliness of this black-faced creature. I had never beheld such a repulsive and extraordinary face before, and yet – if the contradiction is credible – I experienced at the same time an odd feeling that in some way I *had* already encountered exactly the features and gestures that now amazed me. Afterwards it occurred to me that probably I had seen him as I was lifted aboard, and yet that scarcely satisfied my suspicion of a previous acquaintance. Yet how one could have set eyes on so singular a face and have forgotten the precise occasion passed my imagination.

Montgomery's movement to follow me released my attention, and I turned and looked about me at the flush deck of the little schooner. I was already half prepared by the sounds I had heard for what I saw. Certainly I never beheld a deck so dirty. It was littered with scraps of carrot, shreds of green stuff, and indescribable filth. Fastened by chains to the mainmast were a number of grisly staghounds, who now began leaping and barking at me, and by the mizzen a huge puma was cramped in a little iron cage, far too small even to give it turning-room. Further under the starboard bulwark were some big hutches containing a number of rabbits, and a solitary llama was squeezed in a mere box of a cage forward. The dogs were muzzled by leather straps. The only human being on deck was a gaunt and silent sailor at the wheel.

The patched and dirty spankers were tense before the wind, and up aloft the little ship seemed carrying every sail she had. The sky was clear, the sun midway down the western sky; long waves, capped by the breeze with froth, were running with us. We went past the steersman to the taffrail and saw the water come foaming under the stern, and the bubbles go dancing and vanishing in her wake. I turned and surveyed the unsavoury length of the ship.

'Is this an ocean menagerie?' said I.

'Looks like it,' said Montgomery.

'What are these beasts for? Merchandise, curios? Does the

captain think he is going to sell them somewhere in the South Seas?'

'It looks like it, doesn't it?' said Montgomery, and turned towards the wake again.

Suddenly we heard a yelp and a volley of furious blasphemy coming from the companion hatchway, and the deformed man with the black face clambered up hurriedly. He was immediately followed by a heavy red-haired man in a white cap. At the sight of the former the staghounds, who had all tired of barking at me by this time, became furiously excited, howling and leaping against their chains. The black hesitated before them, and this gave the red-haired man time to come up with him and deliver a tremendous blow between the shoulder-blades. The poor devil went down like a felled ox, and rolled in the dirt among the furiously excited dogs. It was lucky for him they were muzzled. The red-haired man gave a yawp of exultation and stood staggering and, as it seemed to me, in serious danger of either going backwards down the companion hatchway, or forwards upon his victim.

So soon as the second man had appeared, Montgomery had started violently. 'Steady on there!' he cried, in a tone of remonstrance. A couple of sailors appeared on the forecastle.

The black-haired man, howling in a singular voice, rolled about under the feet of the dogs. No one attempted to help him. The brutes did their best to worry him, butting their muzzles at him. There was a quick dance of their lithe grey bodies over the clumsy prostrate figure. The sailors forward shouted to them as though it was admirable sport. Montgomery gave an angry exclamation, and went striding down the deck. I followed him.

In another second the black-faced man had scrambled up and was staggering forward. He stumbled up against the bulwark by the main shrouds, where he remained panting and glaring over his shoulder at the dogs. The red-haired man laughed a satisfied laugh.

'Look here, captain,' said Montgomery, with his lisp a little accentuated, gripping the elbows of the red-haired man; 'this won't do.'

I stood behind Montgomery. The captain came half round

and regarded him with the dull and solemn eyes of a drunken man. 'Wha' won't do?' he said; and added, after looking sleepily into Montgomery's face for a minute, 'Blasted Sawbones!'

With a sudden movement he shook his arms free, and after two ineffectual attempts stuck his freckled fists into his side-pockets.

'That man's a passenger,' said Montgomery. 'I'd advise you to keep your hands off him.'

'Go to hell!' said the captain loudly. He suddenly turned and staggered towards the side. 'Do what I like on my own ship,' he said.

I think Montgomery might have left him then – seeing the brute was drunk. But he only turned a shade paler, and followed the captain to the bulwarks.

'Look here, captain,' he said. 'That man of mine is not to be ill-treated. He has been hazed ever since he came aboard.'

For a minute alcoholic fumes kept the captain speechless. 'Blasted Sawbones!' was all he considered necessary.

I could see that Montgomery had one of those slow pertinacious tempers that will warm day after day to a white heat and never again cool to forgiveness, and I saw too that this quarrel had been some time growing. 'The man's drunk,' said I, perhaps officiously; 'you'll do no good.'

Montgomery gave an ugly twist to his dropping lip. 'He's always drunk. Do you think that excuses his assaulting his passengers?'

'My ship,' began the captain, waving his hand unsteadily towards the cages, 'was a clean ship. Look at it now.' It was certainly anything but clean. 'Crew,' continued the captain, 'clean respectable crew.'

'You agreed to take the beasts.'

'I wish I'd never set eyes on your infernal island. What the devil ... want beasts for on an island like that? Then that man of yours ... Understood he was a man. He's a lunatic. And he hadn't no business aft. Do you think the whole damned ship belongs to you?'

'Your sailors began to haze the poor devil as soon as he came aboard.'

'That's just what he is – he's a devil, an ugly devil. My men can't stand him. *I* can't stand him. None of us can't stand him. Nor *you* either.'

Montgomery turned away. '*You* leave that man alone, anyhow,' he said, nodding his head as he spoke.

But the captain meant to quarrel now. He raised his voice : 'If he comes this end of the ship again I'll cut his insides out, I tell you. Cut out his blasted insides ! Who are *you* to tell *me* what *I'm* to do. I tell you I'm captain of the ship – Captain and Owner. I'm the law here, I tell you – the law and the prophets. I bargained to take a man and his attendant to and from Arica and bring back some animals. I never bargained to carry a mad devil and a silly Sawbones, a – '

Well, never mind what he called Montgomery. I saw the latter take a step forward, and interposed. 'He's drunk,' said I. The captain began some abuse even fouler than the last. 'Shut up,' I said, turning on him sharply, for I had seen danger in Montgomery's white face. With that I brought the downpour on myself.

However, I was glad to avert what was uncommonly near a scuffle, even at the price of the captain's drunken ill-will. I do not think I have ever heard quite so much vile language come in a continuous stream from any man's lips before, though I have frequented eccentric company enough. I found some of it hard to endure – though I am a mild-tempered man. But certainly when I told the captain to shut up I had forgotten I was merely a bit of human flotsam, cut off from my resources, and with my fare unpaid, a mere casual dependant on the bounty – or speculative enterprise – of the ship. He reminded me of it with considerable vigour. But at any rate I prevented a fight.

4

At the Schooner's Rail

That night land was sighted after sundown, and the schooner hove to. Montgomery intimated that was his destination. It was too far to see any details; it seemed to me then simply a low-lying patch of dim blue in the uncertain blue-grey sea. An almost vertical streak of smoke went up from it into the sky.

The captain was not on deck when it was sighted. After he had vented his wrath on me he had staggered below, and I understand he went to sleep on the floor of his own cabin. The mate practically assumed the command. He was the gaunt, taciturn individual we had seen at the wheel. Apparently he too was in an evil temper with Montgomery. He took not the slightest notice of either of us. We dined with him in a sulky silence, after a few ineffectual efforts on my part to talk. It struck me, too, that the men regarded my companion and his animals in a singularly unfriendly manner. I found Montgomery very reticent about his purpose with these creatures, and about his destination, and though I was sensible of a growing curiosity I did not press him.

We remained talking on the quarter-deck until the sky was thick with stars. Except for an occasional sound in the yellow-lit forecastle, and a movement of the animals now and then, the night was very still. The puma lay crouched together, watching us with shining eyes, a black heap in the corner of its cage. The dogs seemed to be asleep. Montgomery produced some cigars.

He talked to me of London in a tone of half-painful reminiscence, asking all kinds of questions about changes that had taken place. He spoke like a man who had loved his life there, and had been suddenly and irrevocably cut off from it. I gossiped as well as I could of this and that. All the time the strangeness of him was shaping itself in my mind, and as I talked I peered at his odd pallid face in the dim light of the binnacle lantern behind me. Then I looked out at the darkling sea, where in the dimness his little island was hidden.

This man, it seemed to me, had come out of Immensity merely to save my life. To-morrow he would drop over the side and vanish again out of my existence. Even had it been under commonplace circumstances it would have made me a trifle thoughtful. But in the first place was the singularity of an educated man living on this unknown little island, and coupled with that, the extraordinary nature of his luggage. I found myself repeating the captain's question : What did he want with the beasts ? Why, too, had he pretended they were not his when I had remarked about them at first ? Then again, in his personal attendant there was a bizarre quality that had impressed me profoundly. These circumstances threw a haze of mystery round the man. They laid hold of my imagination and hampered my tongue.

Towards midnight our talk of London died away, and we stood side by side leaning over the bulwarks, and staring dreamily over the silent starlit sea, each pursuing his own thoughts. It was the atmosphere for sentiment, and I began upon my gratitude.

'If I may say it,' said I, after a time, 'you have saved my life.'

'Chance,' he answered ; 'just chance.'

'I prefer to make my thanks to the accessible agent.'

'Thank no one. You had the need, and I the knowledge, and I injected and fed you much as I might have collected a specimen. I was bored, and wanted something to do. If I'd been jaded that day, or hadn't liked your face, well — ; it's a curious question where you would have been now.'

This damped my mood a little. 'At any rate — ' I began.

'It's chance, I tell you,' he interrupted, 'as everything is in a man's life. Only the asses won't see it. Why am I here now — an outcast from civilisation — instead of being a happy man, enjoying all the pleasures of London ? Simply because — eleven years ago — I lost my head for ten minutes on a foggy night.'

He stopped. 'Yes ?' said I.

'That's all.'

We relapsed into silence. Presently he laughed. 'There's something in this starlight that loosens one's tongue. I'm an ass, and yet somehow I would like to tell you.'

'Whatever you tell me, you may rely upon my keeping to myself . . . If that's it.'

He was on the point of beginning, and then shook his head doubtfully. 'Don't,' said I. 'It is all the same to me. After all, it is better to keep your secret. There's nothing gained but a little relief, if I respect your confidence. If I don't . . . well?'

He grunted undecidedly. I felt I had him at a disadvantage, had caught him in the mood of indiscretion; and, to tell the truth, I was not curious to learn what might have driven a young medical student out of London. I have an imagination. I shrugged my shoulders, and turned away. Over the taffrail leant a silent black figure, watching the stars. It was Montgomery's strange attendant. It looked over its shoulder quickly with my movement, then looked away again.

It may seem a little thing to you, perhaps, but it came like a sudden blow to me. The only light near us was a lantern at the wheel. The creature's face was turned for one brief instant out of the dimness of the stern towards this illumination, and I saw that the eyes that glanced at me shone with a pale green light.

I did not know then that a reddish luminosity, at least, is not uncommon in human eyes. The thing came to me as stark inhumanity. That black figure, with its eyes of fire, struck down through all my adult thoughts and feelings, and for a moment the forgotten horrors of childhood came back to my mind. Then the effect passed as it had come. An uncouth black figure of a man, a figure of no particular import, hung over the taffrail, against the starlight, and I found Montgomery was speaking to me.

'I'm thinking of turning in, then,' said he; 'if you've had enough of this.'

I answered him incongruously. We went below, and he wished me good-night at the door of my cabin.

That night I had some very unpleasant dreams. The waning moon rose late. Its light struck a ghostly faint white beam across my cabin, and made an ominous shape on the planking by my bunk. Then the staghounds woke, and began howling and baying, so that I dreamt fitfully, and scarcely slept until the approach of dawn.

5
The Man who had Nowhere to go

In the early morning – it was the second morning after my recovery, and I believe the fourth after I was picked up – I awoke through an avenue of tumultuous dreams, dreams of guns and howling mobs, and became sensible of a hoarse shouting above me. I rubbed my eyes, and lay listening to the noise, doubtful for a little while of my whereabouts. Then came a sudden pattering of bare feet, the sound of heavy objects being thrown about, a violent creaking and rattling of chains. I heard the swish of the water as the ship was suddenly brought round, and a foamy yellow-green wave flew across the little round window and left it streaming. I jumped into my clothes and went on deck.

As I came up the ladder I saw against the flushed sky – for the sun was just rising – the broad back and red hair of the captain, and over his shoulder the puma spinning from a tackle rigged on to the mizzen spanker boom. The poor brute seemed horribly scared, and crouched in the bottom of its little cage. 'Overboard with 'em!' bawled the captain. 'Overboard with 'em! We'll have a clean ship soon of the whole bilin' of 'em.'

He stood in my way, so that I had perforce to tap his shoulder to come on deck. He came round with a start, and staggered back a few paces to stare at me. It needed no expert eye to tell that the man was still drunk. 'Hullo!' said he stupidly, and then with a light coming into his eyes, 'Why, it's Mister – Mister – ?'

'Prendick,' said I.

'Prendick be damned!' said he. 'Shut Up – that's your name. Mister Shut Up!'

It was no good answering the brute. But I certainly did not expect his next move. He held out his hand to the gangway by which Montgomery stood talking to a massive white-haired man in dirty blue flannels, who had apparently just come aboard. 'That way, Mister Blasted Shut Up. That Way,' roared the captain.

Montgomery and his companion turned as he spoke.

'What do you mean?' said I.

'That way, Mister Blasted Shut Up – that's what I mean. Overboard, Mister Shut Up – and sharp. We're clearing the ship out, cleaning the whole blessed ship out. And overboard you go.'

I stared at him dumbfounded. Then it occurred to me it was exactly the thing I wanted. The lost prospect of a journey as sole passenger with this quarrelsome sot was not one to mourn over. I turned towards Montgomery.

'Can't have you,' said Montgomery's companion concisely.

'You can't have me!' said I, aghast. He had the squarest and most resolute face I ever set eyes upon.

'Look here,' I began, turning to the captain.

'Overboard,' said the captain. 'This ship ain't for beasts and cannibals, and worse than beasts, any more. Overboard you go ... Mr Shut Up. If they can't have you, you goes adrift. But anyhow you go! With your Friends. I've done with this blessed island for evermore amen! I've had enough of it.'

'But, Montgomery,' I appealed.

He distorted his lower lip, and nodded his head hopelessly at the grey-haired man beside him, to indicate his powerlessness to help me.

'I'll see to *you* presently,' said the captain.

Then began a curious three-cornered altercation. Alternately I appealed to one and another of the three men, first to the grey-haired man to let me land, and then to the drunken captain to keep me aboard. I even bawled entreaties to the sailors. Montgomery said never a word; only shook his head. 'You're going overboard, I tell you,' was the captain's refrain ... 'Law be damned! I'm king here.'

At last, I must confess, my voice suddenly broke in the middle of a vigorous threat. I felt a gust of hysterical petulance, and went aft, and stared dismally at nothing.

Meanwhile the sailors progressed rapidly with the task of

unshipping the packages and caged animals. A large launch with two standing lugs lay under the lee of the schooner, and into this the strange assortment of goods were swung. I did not then see the hands from the island that were receiving the packages, for the hull of the launch was hidden from me by the side of the schooner.

Neither Montgomery nor his companion took the slightest notice of me, but busied themselves in assisting and directing the four or five sailors who were unloading the goods. The captain went forward, interfering rather than assisting. I was alternately despairful and desperate. Once or twice, as I stood waiting there for things to accomplish themselves, I could not resist an impulse to laugh at my miserable quandary. I felt all the wretcheder for the lack of a breakfast. Hunger and a lack of blood-corpuscles take all the manhood from a man. I perceived pretty clearly that I had not the stamina either to resist what the captain chose to do to expel me, or to force myself upon Montgomery and his companion. So I waited passively upon fate, and the work of transferring Montgomery's possessions to the launch went on as if I did not exist.

Presently that work was finished, and then came a struggle ; I was hauled, resisting weakly enough, to the gangway. Even then I noticed the oddness of the brown faces of the men who were with Montgomery in the launch. But the launch was now fully laden, and was shoved off hastily. A broadening gap of green water appeared under me, and I pushed back with all my strength to avoid falling headlong.

The hands in the launch shouted derisively, and I heard Montgomery curse at them. And then the captain, the mate and one of the seamen helping him, ran me aft towards the stern. The dingey of the *Lady Vain* had been towing behind ; it was half full of water, had no oars, and was quite unvictualled. I refused to go aboard her, and flung myself full-length on the deck. In the end they swung me into her by a rope – for they had no stern ladder, – and then they cut me adrift.

I drifted slowly from the schooner. In a kind of stupor I watched all hands take to the rigging, and slowly but surely she came round to the wind. The sails fluttered, and then bellied out as the wind came into them. I stared at her weather-beaten side heeling steeply towards me. And then she passed out of my range of view.

I did not turn my head to follow her. At first I could scarcely believe what had happened. I crouched in the bottom of the dingey, stunned, and staring blankly at the vacant oily sea. Then I realised I was in that little hell of mine again, now half-swamped. Looking back over the gunwale I saw the schooner standing away from me, with the red-haired captain mocking at me over the taffrail; and, turning towards the island, saw the launch growing smaller as she approached the beach.

Abruptly the cruelty of this desertion became clear to me. I had no means of reaching the land unless I should chance to drift there. I was still weak, you must remember, from my exposure in the boat; I was empty and very faint, or I should have had more heart. But as it was I suddenly began to sob and weep as I had never done since I was a little child. The tears ran down my face. In a passion of despair I struck with my fists at the water in the bottom of the boat, and kicked savagely at the gunwale. I prayed aloud to God that he would let me die.

6

The Evil-looking Boatmen

But the islanders, seeing I was really adrift, took pity on me. I drifted very slowly to the eastward, approaching the island slantingly, and presently I saw with hysterical relief the launch come round and return towards me. She was heavily laden, and as she drew near I could make out Montgomery's white-haired broad-shouldered companion sitting cramped up with the dogs and several packing-cases in the stern sheets. This individual stared fixedly at me without moving or speaking. The black-faced cripple was glaring at me as fixedly in the bows near the puma. There were three other men besides, strange brutish-looking fellows, at whom the staghounds were snarling savagely. Montgomery, who was steering, brought the boat by me, and, rising, caught and fastened my painter to the tiller to tow me – for there was no room aboard.

I had recovered from my hysterical phase by this time, and answered his hail as he approached bravely enough. I told him the dingey was nearly swamped, and he reached me a piggin. I was jerked back as the rope tightened between the boats. For some time I was busy baling.

It was not until I had got the water under – for the water in the dingey had been shipped, the boat was perfectly sound – that I had leisure to look at the people in the launch again.

The white-haired man, I found, was still regarding me stead-fastly, but with an expression, as I now fancied, of some perplexity. When my eyes met his he looked down at the staghound that sat between his knees. He was a powerfully built man, as I have said, with a fine forehead and rather heavy features; but his eyes had that odd drooping of the skin above the lids that often comes with advancing years, and the fall of his heavy mouth at the corners gave him an expression of

pugnacious resolution. He talked to Montgomery in a tone too
low for me to hear. From him my eyes travelled to his three
men, and a strange crew they were. I saw only their faces, yet
there was something in their faces – I knew not what – that gave
me a queer spasm of disgust. I looked steadily at them, and the
impression did not pass, though I failed to see what had
occasioned it. They seemed to me then to be brown men, but
their limbs were oddly swathed in some thin dirty white stuff
down even to the fingers and feet. I have never seen men so
wrapped up before, and women so only in the East. They wore
turbans too, and thereunder peered out their elfin faces at me,
faces with protruding lower jaws and bright eyes. They had lank
black hair, almost like horse-hair, and seemed, as they sat, to
exceed in stature any race of men I have seen. The white-haired
man, who I knew was a good six feet in height, sat a head below
any one of the three. I found afterwards that really none were
taller than myself, but their bodies were abnormally long, and
the thigh-part of the leg short and curiously twisted. At any rate
they were an amazingly ugly gang, and over the heads of them,
under the forward lug, peered the black face of the man whose
eyes were luminous in the dark.

As I stared at them they met my gaze, and then first one and
then another turned away from my direct stare and looked at
me in an odd furtive manner. It occurred to me that I was
perhaps annoying them, and I turned my attention to the island
we were approaching.

It was low, and covered with thick vegetation, chiefly a kind
of palm that was new to me. From one point a thin white thread
of vapour rose slantingly to an immense height, and then frayed
out like a down feather. We were now within the embrace of a
broad bay flanked on either hand by a low promontory. The
beach was of dull grey sand, and sloped steeply up to a ridge,
perhaps sixty or seventy feet above the sea-level, and irregularly
set with trees and undergrowth. Half-way up was a square
piebald stone enclosure that I found subsequently was built
partly of coral and partly of pumiceous lava. Two thatched
roofs peeped from within this enclosure.

A man stood awaiting us at the water's edge. I fancied, while we were still far off, that I saw some other and very grotesque-looking creatures scuttle into the bushes upon the slope, but I saw nothing of these as we drew nearer. This man was of a moderate size, and with a black negroid face. He had a large, almost lipless mouth, extraordinary lank arms, long thin feet and bow legs, and stood with his heavy face thrust forward staring at us. He was dressed like Montgomery and his white-haired companion, in jacket and trousers of blue serge.

As we came still nearer, this individual began to run to and fro on the beach, making the most grotesque movements. At a word of command from Montgomery the four men in the launch sprang up with singular awkward gestures and struck the lugs. Montgomery steered us round and into a narrow little dock excavated in the beach. Then the man on the beach hastened towards us. This dock, as I call it, was really a mere ditch just long enough at this phase of the tide to take the long-boat.

I heard the bows ground in the sand, staved the dingey off the rudder of the big boat with my piggin, and, freeing the painter, landed. The three muffled men, with the clumsiest movements, scrambled out upon the sand, and forthwith set to landing the cargo, assisted by the man on the beach. I was struck especially with the curious movements of the legs of the three swathed and bandaged boatmen – not stiff they were, but distorted in some odd way, almost as if they were jointed in the wrong place. The dogs were still snarling, and strained at their chains after these men, as the white-haired man landed with them.

The three big fellows spoke to one another in odd guttural tones, and the man, who had waited for us on the beach, began chattering to them excitedly – a foreign language, as I fancied – as they laid hands on some bales piled near the stern. Somewhere I had heard such a voice before, and I could not think where. The white-haired man stood holding in a tumult of six dogs, and bawling orders over their din. Montgomery, having unshipped the rudder, landed likewise, and all set to work at unloading. I was too faint, what with my long fast and the sun beating down on my bare head, to offer any assistance.

Presently the white-haired man seemed to recollect my presence, and came up to me. 'You look,' said he, 'as though you had scarcely breakfasted.'

His little eyes were a brilliant black under his heavy brows. 'I must apologise for that. Now you are our guest, we must make you comfortable – though you are uninvited, you know.'

He looked keenly into my face. 'Montgomery says you are an educated man, Mr Prendick – says you know something of science. May I ask what that signifies?'

I told him I had spent some years at the Royal College of Science, and had done some research in biology under Huxley. He raised his eyebrows slightly at that.

'That alters the case a little, Mr Prendick,' he said, with a trifle more respect in his manner. 'As it happens, we are biologists here. This is a biological station – of a sort.' His eye rested on the men in white, who were busily hauling the puma, on rollers, towards the walled yard. 'I and Montgomery, at least,' he added.

Then, 'When you will be able to get away, I can't say. We're off the track to anywhere. We see a ship once in a twelvemonth or so.'

He left me abruptly and went up the beach past this group, and, I think, entered the enclosure. The other two men were with Montgomery erecting a pile of smaller packages on a low wheeled truck. The llama was still on the launch with the rabbit-hutches; the staghounds still lashed to the thwarts. The pile of things completed, all three men laid hold of the truck, and began shoving the ton-weight or so upon it after the puma. Presently Montgomery left them, and coming back to me, held out his hand.

'I'm glad,' said he, 'for my own part. That captain was a silly ass. He'd have made things lively for you.'

'It was you,' said I, 'that saved me again.'

'That depends. You'll find this island an infernally rum place, I promise you. I'd watch my goings carefully if I were you. *He* – ' He hesitated, and seemed to alter his mind about what was on his lips. 'I wish you'd help me with these rabbits,' he said.

His procedure with the rabbits was singular. I waded in with him and helped him lug one of the hutches ashore. No sooner was that done than he opened the door of it, and tilting the thing on one end, turned its living contents out on the ground. They fell in a struggling heap one on the top of the other. He clapped his hands, and forthwith they went off with that hopping run of theirs, fifteen or twenty of them, I should think, up the beach. 'Increase and multiply, my friends,' said Montgomery. 'Replenish the island. Hitherto we've had a certain lack of meat here.'

As I watched them disappearing, the white-haired man returned with a brandy flask and some biscuits. 'Something to go on with, Prendick,' said he in a far more familiar tone than before.

I made no ado, but set to work on the biscuits at once, while the white-haired man helped Montgomery to release about a score more of the rabbits. Three big hutches, however, went up to the house with the puma. The brandy I did not touch, for I have been an abstainer from my birth.

7

The Locked Door

The reader will perhaps understand that at first everything was so strange about me, and my position was the outcome of such unexpected adventures, that I had no discernment of the relative strangeness of this or that thing about me. I followed the llama up the beach, and was overtaken by Montgomery, who asked me not to enter the stone enclosure. I noticed then that the puma in its cage and the pile of packages, had been placed outside the entrance to this quadrangle.

I turned and saw that the launch had now been unloaded, run out again, and was being beached, and the white-haired man was walking towards us. He addressed Montgomery.

'And now comes the problem of this uninvited guest. What are we to do with him?'

'He knows something of science,' said Montgomery.

'I'm itching to get to work again – with this new stuff,' said the grey-haired man, nodding towards the enclosure. His eyes grew brighter.

'I daresay you are,' said Montgomery, in anything but a cordial tone.

'We can't send him over there, and we can't spare the time to build him a new shanty. And we certainly can't take him into our confidence just yet.'

'I'm in your hands,' said I. I had no idea of what he meant by 'over there.'

'I've been thinking of the same things,' Montgomery answered. 'There's my room with the outer door – '

'That's it,' said the elder man promptly, looking at Montgomery, and all three of us went towards the enclosure. 'I'm sorry to make a mystery, Mr Prendick – but you'll remember you're uninvited. Our little establishment here contains a secret or so, is a kind of Bluebeard's Chamber, in fact. Nothing very dreadful really – to a sane man. But just now – as we don't know you –'

'Decidedly,' said I; 'I should be a fool to take offence at any want of confidence.'

He twisted his heavy mouth into a faint smile – he was one of those saturnine people who smile with the corners of the mouth down, – and bowed his acknowledgment of my complaisance. The main entrance to the enclosure we passed; it was a heavy wooden gate, framed in iron and locked, with the cargo of the launch piled outside it; and at the corner we came to a small doorway I had not previously observed. The grey-haired man produced a bundle of keys from the pocket of his greasy blue jacket, opened this door, and entered. His keys and the elaborate locking up of the place, even while it was still under his eye, struck me as peculiar.

I followed him, and found myself in a small apartment, plainly but not uncomfortably furnished, and with its inner door, which was slightly ajar, opening into a paved courtyard. This inner door Montgomery at once closed. A hammock was slung across the darker corner of the room, and a small unglazed window, defended by an iron bar, looked out towards the sea.

This, the grey-haired man told me, was to be my apartment, and the inner door, which, 'for fear of accidents,' he said, he would lock on the other side, was my limit inward. He called my attention to a convenient deck-chair before the window, and to an array of old books, chiefly, I found, surgical works and editions of the Latin and Greek classics – languages I cannot read with any comfort – on a shelf near the hammock. He left the room by the outer door, as if to avoid opening the inner one again.

'We usually have our meals in here,' said Montgomery, and then, as if in doubt, went out after the other. 'Moreau,' I heard him call, and for the moment I do not think I noticed. Then as I handled the books on the shelf it came up in consciousness: where had I heard the name of Moreau before?

I sat down before the window, took out the biscuits that still remained with me, and ate them with an excellent appetite. 'Moreau?'

Through the window I saw one of those unaccountable men in white lugging a packing-case along the beach. Presently the windowframe hid him. Then I heard a key inserted and turned in the lock behind me. After a little while I heard, through the locked door, the noise of the staghounds, which had now been brought up from the beach. They were not barking, but sniffing and growling in a curious fashion. I could hear the rapid patter of their feet, and Montgomery's voice soothing them.

I was very much impressed by the elaborate secrecy of these two men regarding the contents of the place, and for some time I was thinking of that, and of the unaccountable familiarity of the name of Moreau. But so odd is the human memory, that I could not then recall that well-known name in its proper connection. From that my thoughts went to the indefinable queerness of the deformed and white-swathed man on the beach. I never saw such a gait, such odd motions, as he pulled at the box. I recalled that none of these men had spoken to me, though most of them I had found looking at me at one time or another in a peculiar furtive manner, quite unlike the frank stare of your unsophisticated savage. I wondered what language they spoke. They had all seemed remarkably taciturn, and when they did speak, endowed with very uncanny voices. What was wrong with them? Then I recalled the eyes of Montgomery's ungainly attendant.

Just as I was thinking of him, he came in. He was now dressed in white, and carried a little tray with some coffee and boiled vegetables thereon. I could hardly repress a shuddering recoil as he came, bending amiably, and placed the tray before me on the table.

Then astonishment paralysed me. Under his stringy black locks I saw his ear! It jumped upon me suddenly, close to my face. The man had pointed ears, covered with a fine brown fur!

'Your breakfast, sair,' he said. I stared at his face without attempting to answer him. He turned and went towards the door, regarding me oddly over his shoulder.

I followed him out with my eyes, and as I did so, by some

trick of unconscious cerebration, there came surging into my head the phrase : 'The Moreau – Hollows' was it ? 'The Moreau – ?' Ah ! it sent my memory back ten years. 'The Moreau Horrors.' The phrase drifted loose in my mind for a moment, and then I saw it in red lettering on a little buff-coloured pamphlet, that to read made one shiver and creep. Then I remembered distinctly all about it. That long-forgotten pamphlet came back with startling vividness to my mind. I had been a mere lad then, and Moreau was, I suppose, about fifty; a prominent and masterful physiologist, well known in scientific circles for his extraordinary imagination and his brutal directness in discussion. Was this the same Moreau ? He had published some very astonishing facts in connection with the transfusion of blood, and, in addition, was known to be doing valuable work on morbid growths. Then suddenly his career was closed. He had to leave England. A journalist obtained access to his laboratory in the capacity of a laboratory assistant, with the deliberate intention of making sensational exposures; and by the help of a shocking accident – if it was an accident – his gruesome pamphlet became notorious. On the day of its publication, a wretched dog, flayed and otherwise mutilated, escaped from Moreau's house.

It was in the silly season, and a prominent editor, a cousin of the temporary laboratory assistant, appealed to the conscience of the nation. It was not the first time that conscience has turned against the methods of research. The doctor was simply howled out of the country. It may be he deserved to be, but I still think the tepid support of his fellow-investigators, and his desertion by the great body of scientific workers, was a shameful thing. Yet some of his experiments, by the journalist's account, were wantonly cruel. He might perhaps have purchased his social peace by abandoning his investigations, but he apparently preferred the latter, as most men would who have once fallen under the overmastering spell of research. He was unmarried, and had indeed nothing but his own interests to consider . . .

I felt convinced that this must be the same man. Everything pointed to it. It dawned upon me to what end the puma and the other animals, which had now been brought with other luggage

into the enclosure behind the house, were destined; and a
curious faint odour, the halitus of something familiar, an odour
that had been in the background of my consciousness hitherto,
suddenly came forward into the forefront of my thoughts. It
was the antiseptic odour of the operating-room. I heard the
puma growling through the wall, and one of the dogs yelped as
though it had been struck.

Yet surely, and especially to another scientific man, there was
nothing so horrible in vivisection as to account for this secrecy.
And by some odd leap in my thoughts the pointed ears and
luminous eyes of Montgomery's attendant came back again
before me with the sharpest definition. I stared before me out at
the green sea, frothing under a freshening breeze, and let these
and other strange memories of the last few days chase each
other through my mind.

What could it mean? A locked enclosure on a lonely island, a
notorious vivisector, and these crippled and distorted men? . . .

8

The Crying of the Puma

Montgomery interrupted my tangle of mystification and suspicion about one, and his grotesque attendant followed him with a tray bearing bread, some herbs, and other eatables, a flask of whisky, a jug of water, and three glasses and knives. I glanced askance at this strange creature, and found him watching me with his queer restless eyes. Montgomery said he would lunch with me, but that Moreau was too pre-occupied with some work to come.

'Moreau!' said I; 'I know that name.'

'The devil you do!' said he. 'What an ass I was to mention it to you. I might have thought. Anyhow, it will give you an inkling of our – mysteries. Whisky?'

'No thanks – I'm an abstainer.'

'I wish I'd been. But it's no use locking the door after the steed is stolen. It was that infernal stuff led to my coming here. That and a foggy night. I thought myself in luck at the time when Moreau offered to get me off. It's queer . . .'

'Montgomery,' said I suddenly, as the outer door closed; 'why has your man pointed ears?'

'Damn!' he said, over his first mouthful of food. He stared at me for a moment, and then repeated, 'Pointed ears?'

'Little points to them,' said I, as calmly as possible, with a catch in my breath; 'and a fine black fur at the edges.'

He helped himself to whisky and water with great deliberation. 'I was under the impression . . . that his hair covered his ears.'

'I saw them as he stooped by me to put that coffee you sent to me on the table. And his eyes shine in the dark.'

By this time Montgomery had recovered from the surprise of my question. 'I always thought,' he said deliberately, with a certain accentuation of his flavouring of lisp; 'that there *was* something the matter with his ears. From the way he covered them . . . What were they like?'

I was persuaded from his manner that this ignorance was a pretence. Still I could hardly tell the man I thought him a liar. 'Pointed,' I said; 'rather small and furry — distinctly furry. But the whole man is one of the strangest beings I ever set eyes on.'

A sharp, hoarse cry of animal pain came from the enclosure behind us. Its depth and volume testified to the puma. I saw Montgomery wince.

'Yes?' he said.

'Where did you pick the creature up?'

'Er — San Francisco . . . He's an ugly brute, I admit. Half-witted, you know. Can't remember where he came from. But I'm used to him, you know. We both are. How does he strike you?'

'He's unnatural,' I said. 'There's something about him . . . Don't think me fanciful, but it gives me a nasty little sensation, a tightening of my muscles, when he comes near me. It's a touch . . . of the diabolical, in fact.'

Montgomery had stopped eating while I told him this. 'Rum,' he said. '*I* can't see it.'

He resumed his meal. 'I had no idea of it,' he said, and masticated. 'The crew of the schooner . . . must have felt it the same . . . Made a dead set at the poor devil . . . You saw the captain?'

Suddenly the puma howled again, this time more painfully. Montgomery swore under his breath. I had half a mind to attack him about the men on the beach. Then the poor brute within gave vent to a series of short, sharp screams.

'Your men on the beach,' said I; 'what race are they?'

'Excellent fellows, aren't they?' said he absent-mindedly, knitting his brows as the animal yelled out sharply. I said no more. There was another outcry worse than the former. He looked at me with his dull grey eyes, and then took some more whisky. He tried to draw me into a discussion about alcohol, professing to have saved my life with it. He seemed anxious to lay stress on the fact that I owed my life to him. I answered him distractedly. Presently our meal came to an end, the misshapen monster with the pointed ears cleared away, and Montgomery left me alone in the room again. All the time he was in a state of ill-concealed irritation at the noise of the vivisected puma. He spoke of his odd want of nerve, and left me to the obvious application.

I found myself that the cries were singularly irritating, and they grew in depth and intensity as the afternoon wore on. They were painful at first, but their constant resurgence at last altogether upset my balance. I flung aside a crib of Horace I had been reading, and began to clench my fists, to bite my lips, and pace the room.

Presently I got to stopping my ears with my fingers.

The emotional appeal of those yells grew upon me steadily, grew at last to such an exquisite expression of suffering that I could stand it in that confined room no longer. I stepped out of the door into the slumberous heat of the late afternoon, and walking past the main entrance – locked again I noticed – turned the corner of the wall.

The crying sounded even louder out of doors. It was as if all the pain in the world had found a voice. Yet had I known such a pain was in the next room, and had it been dumb, I believe – I have thought since – I could have stood it well enough. It is when suffering finds a voice and sets our nerves quivering that this pity comes troubling us. But in spite of the brilliant sunlight and the green fans of the trees waving in the soothing sea-breeze, the world was a confusion, blurred with drifting black and red phantasms, until I was out of earshot of the house in the chequered wall.

9

The Thing in the Forest

I strode through the undergrowth that clothed the ridge behind the house, scarcely heeding whither I went, passed on through the shadow of a thick cluster of straight-stemmed trees beyond it, and so presently found myself some way on the other side of the ridge, and descending towards a streamlet that ran through a narrow valley. I paused and listened. The distance I had come, or the intervening masses of thicket, deadened any sound that might be coming from the enclosure. The air was still. Then with a rustle a rabbit emerged, and went scampering up the slope before me. I hesitated, and sat down in the edge of the shade.

The place was a pleasant one. The rivulet was hidden by the luxuriant vegetation of the banks, save at one point, where I caught a triangular patch of its glittering water. On the further side I saw through a bluish haze a tangle of trees and creepers, and above these again the luminous blue of the sky. Here and there a splash of white or crimson marked the blooming of some trailing epiphyte. I let my eyes wander over this scene for a while, and then began to turn over in my mind again the strange peculiarities of Montgomery's man. But it was too hot to think elaborately, and presently I fell into a tranquil state midway between dozing and waking.

From this I was aroused, after I know not how long, by a rustling amidst the greenery on the other side of the stream. For a moment I could see nothing but the waving summits of the ferns and reeds. Then suddenly upon the bank of the stream appeared something – at first I could not distinguish what it was. It bowed its head to the water and began to drink. Then I saw it was a man, going on all-fours like a beast!

He was clothed in bluish cloth, and was of a copper-coloured hue, with black hair. It seemed that grotesque ugliness was an invariable character of these islanders. I could hear the suck of the water at his lips as he drank.

I leant forward to see him better, and a piece of lava, detached by my hand, went pattering down the slope. He looked up guiltily, and his eyes met mine. Forthwith he scrambled to his feet and stood wiping his clumsy hand across his mouth and regarding me. His legs were scarcely half the length of his body. So, staring one another out of countenance, we remained for perhaps the space of a minute. Then, stopping to look back once or twice, he slunk off among the bushes to the right of me, and I heard the swish of the fronds grow faint in the distance and die away. Every now and then he regarded me with a steadfast stare. Long after he had disappeared I remained sitting up staring in the direction of his retreat. My drowsy tranquillity had gone.

I was startled by a noise behind me, and, turning suddenly, saw the flapping white tail of a rabbit vanishing up the slope. I jumped to my feet.

The apparition of this grotesque half-bestial creature had suddenly populated the stillness of the afternoon for me. I looked around me rather nervously, and regretted that I was unarmed. Then I thought that the man I had just seen had been clothed in bluish cloth, had not been naked as a savage would have been, and I tried to persuade myself from the fact that he was after all probably a peaceful character, that the dull ferocity of his countenance belied him.

Yet I was greatly disturbed at the apparition. I walked to the left along the slope, turning my head about and peering this way and that among the straight stems of the trees. Why should a man go on all-fours and drink with his lips? Presently I heard an animal wailing again, and taking it to be the puma, I turned about and walked in a direction diametrically opposite to the sound. This led me down to the stream, across which I stepped and pushed my way up through the undergrowth beyond.

I was startled by a great patch of vivid scarlet on the ground, and going up to it found it to be a peculiar fungus branched and corrugated like a foliaceous lichen, but deliquescing into slime at the touch. And then in the shadow of some luxuriant ferns I came upon an unpleasant thing, the dead body of a rabbit, covered with shining flies, but still warm, and with the head torn off. I stopped aghast at the sight of the scattered blood. Here at least was one visitor to the island disposed of!

There were no traces of other violence about it. It looked as though it had been suddenly snatched up and killed. And as I stared at the little furry body came the difficulty of how the thing had been done. The vague dread that had been in my mind since I had seen the inhuman face of the man at the stream grew distincter as I stood there. I began to realise the hardihood of my expedition among these unknown people. The thicket about me became altered to my imagination. Every shadow became something more than a shadow, became an ambush, every rustle became a threat. Invisible things seemed watching me.

I resolved to go back to the enclosure on the beach. I suddenly turned away and thrust myself violently – possibly even frantically – through the bushes, anxious to get a clear space about me again.

I stopped just in time to prevent myself emerging upon an open space. It was a kind of glade in the forest made by a fall; seedlings were already starting up to struggle for the vacant space, and beyond, the dense growth of stems and twining vines and splashes of fungus and flowers closed in again. Before me, squatting together upon the fungoid ruins of a huge fallen tree, and still unaware of my approach, were three grotesque human figures. One was evidently a female. The other two were men. They were naked, save for swathings of scarlet cloth about the middles, and their skins were of a dull pinkish drab colour, such as I had seen in no savages before. They had fat heavy chinless faces, retreating foreheads, and a scant bristly hair upon their heads. Never before had I seen such bestial-looking creatures.

They were talking, or at least one of the men was talking to the other two, and all three had been too closely interested to heed the rustling of my approach. They swayed their heads and shoulders from side to side. The speaker's words came thick and sloppy, and though I could hear them distinctly I could not distinguish what he said. He seemed to me to be reciting some complicated gibberish. Presently his articulation became shriller, and spreading his hands he rose to his feet.

At that the others began to gibber in unison, also rising to their feet, spreading their hands, and swaying their bodies in rhythm with their chant. I noticed then the abnormal shortness of their legs and their lank clumsy feet. All three began slowly to circle round, raising and stamping their feet and waving their arms; a kind of tune crept into their rhythmic recitation, and a refrain – 'Aloola' or 'Baloola' it sounded like. Their eyes began to sparkle and their ugly faces to brighten with an expression of strange pleasure. Saliva dropped from their lipless mouths.

Suddenly, as I watched their grotesque and unaccountable gestures, I perceived clearly for the first time what it was that had offended me, what had given me the two inconsistent and conflicting impressions of utter strangeness and yet of the strangest familiarity. The three creatures engaged in this mysterious rite were human in shape, and yet human beings with the strangest air about them of some familiar animal. Each of these creatures, despite its human form, its rag of clothing, and the rough humanity of its bodily form, had woven into it, into its movements, into the expression of its countenance, into its whole presence, some now irresistible suggestion of a hog, a swinish taint, the unmistakable mark of the beast.

I stood overcome by this amazing realisation, and then the most horrible questionings came rushing into my mind. They began leaping into the air, first one and then the other, whooping and grunting. Then one slipped, and for a moment was on all-fours, to recover indeed forthwith. But that transitory gleam of the true animalism of these monsters was enough.

I turned as noiselessly as possible, and becoming every now and then rigid with the fear of being discovered as a branch cracked or a leaf rustled, I pushed back into the bushes. It was long before I grew bolder and dared to move freely.

My one idea for the moment was to get away from these foul beings, and I scarcely noticed that I had emerged upon a faint pathway amidst the trees. Then, suddenly traversing a little glade, I saw with an unpleasant start two clumsy legs among the trees, walking with noiseless footsteps parallel with my course, and perhaps thirty yards away from me. The head and upper part of the body were hidden by a tangle of creeper. I stopped abruptly, hoping the creature did not see me. The feet stopped as I did. So nervous was I that I controlled an impulse to headlong flight with the utmost difficulty.

Then, looking hard, I distinguished through the interlacing network the head and body of the brute I had seen drinking. He moved his head. There was an emerald flash in his eyes as he glanced at me from the shadow of the trees, a half-luminous colour, that vanished as he turned his head again. He was motionless for a moment, and then with noiseless tread began running through the green confusion. In another moment he had vanished behind some bushes. I could not see him, but I felt that he had stopped and was watching me again.

What on earth was he – man or animal? What did he want with me? I had no weapon, not even a stick. Flight would be madness. At any rate the Thing, whatever it was, lacked the courage to attack me. Setting my teeth hard I walked straight towards him. I was anxious not to show the fear that seemed chilling my backbone. I pushed through a tangle of tall white-flowered bushes, and saw him twenty yards beyond, looking over his shoulder at me and hesitating. I advanced a step or two looking steadfastly into his eyes.

'Who are you?' said I. He tried to meet my gaze.

'No!' he said suddenly, and, turning, went bounding away from me through the undergrowth. Then he turned and stared at me again. His eyes shone brightly out of the dusk under the trees.

My heart was in my mouth, but I felt my only chance was bluff, and walked steadily towards him. He turned again and vanished into the dusk. Once more I thought I caught the glint of his eyes, and that was all.

For the first time I realised how the lateness of the hour might affect me. The sun had set some minutes since, the swift dusk of the tropics was already fading out of the eastern sky, and a pioneer moth fluttered silently by my head. Unless I would spend the night among the unknown dangers of the mysterious forest, I must hasten back to the enclosure.

The thought of a return to that pain-haunted refuge was extremely disagreeable, but still more so was the idea of being overtaken in the open by darkness, and all that darkness might conceal. I gave one more look into the blue shadows that had swallowed up this odd creature, and then retraced my way down the slope towards the stream, going as I judged in the direction from which I had come.

I walked eagerly, perplexed by all these things, and presently found myself in a level place among scattered trees. The colourless clearness that comes after the sunset flush was darkling. The blue sky above grew momentarily deeper, and the little stars one by one pierced the attenuated light; the interspaces of the trees, the gaps in the further vegetation, that had been hazy blue in the daylight, grew black and mysterious.

I pushed on. The colour vanished from the world, the tree-tops rose against the luminous blue sky in inky silhouette, and all below that outline melted into one formless blackness. Presently the trees grew thinner, and the shrubby undergrowth more abundant. Then there was a desolate space covered with white sand, and then another expanse of tangled bushes.

I was tormented by a faint rustling upon my right hand. I thought at first it was fancy, for whenever I stopped, there was silence, save for the evening breeze in the tree-tops. Then when I went on again there was an echo to my footsteps.

I moved away from the thickets, keeping to the more open ground, and endeavouring by sudden turns now and then to surprise this thing, if it existed, in the act of creeping upon me. I saw nothing, and nevertheless my sense of another presence grew steadily. I increased my pace, and after some time came to a slight ridge, crossed it and turned sharply, regarding it steadfastly from the further side. It came out black and clear-cut against the darkling sky.

And presently a shapeless lump heaved up momentarily against the skyline and vanished again. I felt assured now that my tawny-faced antagonist was stalking me again. And coupled with that was another unpleasant realisation, that I had lost my way.

For a time I hurried on hopelessly perplexed, pursued by that stealthy approach. Whatever it was, the thing either lacked the courage to attack me, or it was waiting to take me at some disadvantage. I kept studiously to the open. At times I would turn and listen, and presently I half-persuaded myself that my pursuer had abandoned the chase, or was a mere creation of my disordered imagination. Then I heard the sound of the sea. I quickened my footsteps almost to a run, and immediately there was a stumble in my rear.

I turned suddenly and stared at the uncertain trees behind me. One black shadow seemed to leap into another. I listened rigid, and heard nothing but the creep of the blood in my ears. I thought that my nerves were unstrung, and that my imagination was tricking me, and turned resolutely towards the sound of the sea again.

In a minute or so the trees grew thinner, and I emerged upon a bare low headland running out into the sombre water. The night was calm and clear, and the reflection of the growing multitude of the stars shivered in the tranquil heaving of the sea. Some way out, the wash upon an irregular band of reef shone with a pallid light of its own. Westward I saw the zodiacal light mingling with the yellow brilliance of the evening star. The coast fell away from me to the east, and westward it was hidden by the shoulder of the cape. Then I recalled the fact that Moreau's beach lay to the west.

A twig snapped behind me and there was a rustle. I turned and stood facing the dark trees. I could see nothing – or else I could see too much. Every dark form in the dimness had its ominous quality, its peculiar suggestion of alert watchfulness. So I stood for perhaps a minute, and then, with an eye to the trees still, turned westward to cross the headland. And as I moved, one among the lurking shadows moved to follow me.

My heart beat quickly. Presently the broad sweep of a bay to the westward became visible, and I halted again. The noiseless shadow halted a dozen yards from me. A little point of light shone on the further bend of the curve, and the grey sweep of the sandy beach lay faint under the starlight. Perhaps two miles away was that little point of light. To get to the beach I should have to go through the trees where the shadows lurked, and down a bushy slope.

I could see the thing rather more distinctly now. It was no animal, for it stood erect. At that I opened my mouth to speak, and found a hoarse phlegm choked my voice. I tried again, and shouted, 'Who is there?' There was no answer. I advanced a step. The thing did not move; only gathered itself together. My foot struck a stone.

That gave me an idea. Without taking my eyes off the black form before me I stooped and picked up this lump of rock. But at my motion the thing turned abruptly as a dog might have done, and slunk obliquely into the further darkness. Then I recalled a schoolboy expedient against big dogs, twisted the rock into my handkerchief, and gave this a turn round my wrist. I heard a movement further off among the shadows as if the thing was in retreat. Then suddenly my tense excitement gave way; I broke into a profuse perspiration and fell a-trembling, with my adversary routed and this weapon in my hand.

It was some time before I could summon resolution to go down through the trees and bushes upon the flank of the headland to the beach. At last I did it at a run, and as I emerged from the thicket upon the sand I heard some other body come crashing after me.

At that I completely lost my head with fear, and began running along the sand. Forthwith there came the swift patter of soft feet in pursuit. I gave a wild cry and redoubled my pace. Some dim black things about three or four times the size of rabbits went running or hopping up from the beach towards the bushes as I passed. So long as I live I shall remember the terror of that chase. I ran near the water's edge, and heard every now and then the splash of the feet that gained upon me. Far away, hopelessly far, was the yellow light. All the night about us was black and still. Splash, splash came the pursuing feet nearer and nearer. I felt my breath going, for I was quite out of training; it whooped as I drew it, and I felt a pain like a knife at my side. I perceived the thing would come up with me long before I reached the enclosure, and, desperate and sobbing for breath, I wheeled round upon it and struck it as it came up to me – struck with all my strength. The stone came out of the sling of the handkerchief as I did so.

As I turned, the thing, which had been running on all-fours, rose to its feet, and the missile fell fair on its left temple. The skull rang loud and the animal-man blundered into me, thrust me back with its hands, and went staggering past me to fall headlong upon the sand with its face in the water. And there it lay still.

I could not bring myself to approach that black heap. I left it there with the water rippling round it under the still stars, and, giving it a wide berth, pursued my way towards the yellow glow of the house. And presently, with a positive effect of relief, came the pitiful moaning of the puma, the sound that had originally driven me out to explore this mysterious island. At that, though I was faint and horribly fatigued, I gathered together all my strength, and began running again towards the light. It seemed to me a voice was calling me.

10

The Crying of the Man

As I drew near the house I saw that the light shone from the open door of my room; and then I heard, coming from out the darkness at the side of that orange oblong, the voice of Montgomery shouting 'Prendick.'

I continued running. Presently I heard him again. I replied by a feeble 'Hullo!' and in another moment had staggered up to him.

'Where have you been?' said he, holding me at arms-length, so that the light from the door fell on my face. 'We have both been so busy that we forgot you until about half an hour ago.'

He led me into the room and sat me down in the deck chair. For a while I was blinded by the light. 'We did not think you would start to explore this island of ours without telling us,' he said. And then, 'I was afraid! But . . . what . . . Hullo!'

For my last remaining strength slipped from me, and my head fell forward on my chest. I think he found a certain satisfaction in giving me brandy. 'For God's sake,' said I, 'fasten that door.'

'You've been meeting some of our curiosities, eh?' said he. He locked the door and turned to me again. He asked me no questions, but gave me some more brandy and water, and pressed me to eat. I was in a state of collapse. He said something vague about his forgetting to warn me, and asked me briefly when I left the house and what I had seen. I answered him as briefly in fragmentary sentences. 'Tell me what it all means,' said I, in a state bordering on hysterics.

'It's nothing so very dreadful,' said he. 'But I think you have had about enough for one day.' The puma suddenly gave a sharp yell of pain. At that he swore under his breath. 'I'm damned,' said he, 'if this place is not as bad as Gower Street — with its cats.'

'Montgomery,' said I, 'what was that thing that came after me. Was it a beast, or was it a man?'

'If you don't sleep to-night,' he said, 'you'll be off your head to-morrow.'

I stood up in front of him. 'What was that thing that came after me?' I asked.

He looked me squarely in the eyes and twisted his mouth askew. His eyes, which had seemed animated a minute before, went dull. 'From your account,' said he, 'I'm thinking it was a bogle.'

I felt a gust of intense irritation that passed as quickly as it came. I flung myself into the chair again and pressed my hands on my forehead. The puma began again.

Montgomery came round behind me and put his hand on my shoulder. 'Look here, Prendick,' he said; 'I had no business to let you drift out into this silly island of ours. But it's not so bad as you feel, man. Your nerves are worked to rags. Let me give you something that will make you sleep. *That* . . . will keep on for hours yet. You must simply get to sleep, or I won't answer for it.'

I did not reply. I bowed forward and covered my face with my hands. Presently he returned with a small measure containing a dark liquid. This he gave me. I took it unresistingly, and he helped me into the hammock.

When I awoke it was broad day. For a little while I lay flat, staring at the roof above me. The rafters, I observed, were made out of the timbers of a ship. Then I turned my head and saw a meal prepared for me on the table. I perceived that I was hungry, and prepared to clamber out of the hammock, which, very politely, anticipating my intention, twisted round and deposited me upon all-fours on the floor.

I got up and sat down before the food. I had a heavy feeling in my head, and only the vaguest memory at first of the things that had happened overnight. The morning breeze blew very pleasantly through the unglazed window, and that and the food contributed to the sense of animal comfort I experienced. Presently the door behind me, the door inward towards the yard of the enclosure, opened. I turned and saw Montgomery's face.

'All right?' said he. 'I'm frightfully busy.' And he shut the door. Afterwards I discovered that he forgot to re-lock it.

Then I recalled the expression of his face the previous night, and with that the memory of all I had experienced reconstructed itself before me. Even as that fear returned to me came a cry from within. But this time it was not the cry of a puma.

I put down the mouthful that hesitated upon my lips, and listened. Silence, save for the whisper of the morning breeze. I began to think my ears had deceived me.

After a long pause I resumed my meal, but with my ears still vigilant. Presently I heard something else very faint and low. I sat as if frozen in my attitude. Though it was faint and low, it moved me more profoundly than all that I had hitherto heard of the abominations behind the wall. There was no mistake this time in the quality of the dim broken sounds, no doubt at all of their source; for it was groaning, broken by sobs and gasps of anguish. It was no brute this time. It was a human being in torment!

And as I realised this I rose, and in three steps had crossed the room, seized the handle of the door into the yard, and flung it open before me.

'Prendick, man! Stop!' cried Montgomery, intervening. A startled deerhound yelped and snarled. There was blood, I saw, in the sink, brown, and some scarlet, and I smelt the peculiar smell of carbolic acid. Then through an open doorway beyond, in the dim light of the shadow, I saw something bound painfully upon a framework, scarred, red, and bandaged. And then blotting this out appeared the face of old Moreau, white and terrible.

In a moment he had gripped me by the shoulder with a hand that was smeared red, had twisted me off my feet, and flung me headlong back into my own room. He lifted me as though I was a little child. I fell at full length upon the floor, and the door slammed and shut out the passionate intensity of his face. Then I heard the key turn in the lock, and Montgomery's voice in expostulation.

'Ruin the work of a lifetime!' I heard Moreau say.

'He does not understand,' said Montgomery, and other things that were inaudible.

'I can't spare the time yet,' said Moreau.

The rest I did not hear. I picked myself up and stood trembling, my mind a chaos of the most horrible misgivings. Could it be possible, I thought, that such a thing as the vivisection of men was possible ? The question shot like lightning across a tumultuous sky. And suddenly the clouded horror of my mind condensed into a vivid realisation of my danger.

11

The Hunting of the Man

It came before my mind with an unreasonable hope of escape, that the outer door of my room was still open to me. I was convinced now, absolutely assured, that Moreau had been vivisecting a human being. All the time since I had heard his name I had been trying to link in my mind in some way the grotesque animalism of the islanders with his abominations; and now I thought I saw it all. The memory of his works in the transfusion of blood recurred to me. These creatures I had seen were the victims of some hideous experiment!

These sickening scoundrels had merely intended to keep me back, to fool me with their display of confidence, and presently to fall upon me with a fate more horrible than death, with torture, and after torture the most hideous degradation it was possible to conceive – to send me off, a lost soul, a beast, to the rest of their Comus rout. I looked round for some weapon. Nothing. Then, with an inspiration, I turned over the deck chair, put my foot on the side of it, and tore away the side rail. It happened that a nail came away with the wood, and, projecting, gave a touch of danger to an otherwise petty weapon. I heard a step outside, incontinently flung open the door, and found Montgomery within a yard of it. He meant to lock the outer door.

I raised this nailed stick of mine and cut at his face, but he sprang back. I hesitated a moment, then turned and fled round the corner of the house. 'Prendick, man!' I heard his astonished cry. 'Don't be a silly ass, man!'

Another minute, thought I, and he would have had me locked in, and as ready as a hospital rabbit for my fate. He emerged behind the corner, for I heard him shout, 'Prendick!' Then he began to run after me, shouting things as he ran.

This time, running blindly, I went north-eastward, in a direction at right angles to my previous expedition. Once, as I went running headlong up the beach, I glanced over my shoulder and saw his attendant with him. I ran furiously up the slope, over it, then turned eastward along a rocky valley, fringed on either side with jungle. I ran for perhaps a mile altogether, my chest straining, my heart beating in my ears, and then, hearing nothing of Montgomery or his man, and feeling upon the verge of exhaustion, I doubled sharply back towards the beach, as I judged, and lay down in the shelter of a cane break.

There I remained for a long time, too fearful to move, and indeed too fearful even to plan a course of action. The wild scene about me lay sleeping silently under the sun, and the only sound near me was the thin hum of some small gnats that had discovered me. Presently I became aware of a drowsy breathing sound – the soughing of the sea upon the beach.

After about an hour I heard Montgomery shouting my name far away to the north. As I interpreted it then, this island was inhabited only by these two vivisectors and their animalised victims. Some of these, no doubt, they could press into their service against me, if need arose. I knew both Moreau and Montgomery carried revolvers; and, save for a feeble bar of deal, spiked with a small nail, the merest mockery of a mace, I was unarmed.

So I lay still where I was until I began to think of food and drink. And at that moment the real hopelessness of my position came home to me. I knew no way of getting anything to eat; I was too ignorant of botany to discover any resort of root or fruit that might lie about me; I had no means of trapping the few rabbits upon the island. It grew blanker the more I turned the prospect over. At last, in the desperation of my position, my mind turned to the animal men I had encountered. I tried to find some hope in what I remembered of them. In turn I recalled each one I had seen, and tried to draw some augury of assistance from my memory.

Then suddenly I heard a staghound bay, and at that realised a new danger. I took little time to think, or they would have caught me then, but, snatching up my nailed stick, rushed headlong from my hiding-place towards the sound of the sea. I remember a growth of thorny plants with spines that stabbed like penknives. I emerged, bleeding, and with torn clothes, upon the lip of a long creek opening northward. I went straight into the waves without a minute's hesitation, wading up the creek, and presently finding myself knee-deep in a little stream. I scrambled out at last on the westward bank, and, with my heart beating loudly in my ears, crept into a tangle of ferns to await the issue. I heard the dog – it was only one – draw nearer, and yelp when it came to the thorns. Then I heard no more, and presently began to think I had escaped.

The minutes passed, the silence lengthened out, and at last, after an hour of security, my courage began to return to me.

By this time I was no longer very terrified or very miserable. For I had, as it were, passed the limit of terror and despair. I felt now that my life was practically lost, and that persuasion made me capable of daring anything. I had even a certain wish to encounter Moreau face to face. And, as I had waded into the water, I remembered that if I were too hard pressed at least one path of escape from torment still lay open to me – they could not very well prevent my drowning myself. I had half a mind to drown myself then, but an odd wish to see the whole adventure out, a queer impersonal spectacular interest in myself, restrained me. I stretched my limbs, sore and painful from the pricks of the spiny plants, and stared around me at the trees; and, so suddenly that it seemed to jump out of the green tracery about it, my eyes lit upon a black face watching me.

I saw that it was the simian creature who had met the launch upon the beach. He was clinging to the oblique stem of a palm-tree. I gripped my stick, and stood up facing him. He began chattering. 'You, you, you,' was all I could distinguish at first. Suddenly he dropped from the tree, and in another moment was holding the fronds apart, and staring curiously at me.

I did not feel the same repugnance towards this creature that I had experienced in my encounters with the other Beast Men. 'You,' he said, 'in the boat.' He was a man, then – at least, as much of a man as Montgomery's attendant – for he could talk.

'Yes,' I said, 'I came in the boat. From the ship.'

'Oh!' he said, and his bright restless eyes travelled over me, to my hands, to the stick I carried, to my feet, to the tattered places in my coat, and the cuts and scratches I had received from the thorns. He seemed puzzled at something. His eyes came back to my hands. He held his own hand out, and counted his digits slowly, 'One, Two, Three, Four, Five – eh?'

I did not grasp his meaning then. Afterwards I was to find that a great proportion of these Beast People had malformed hands, lacking sometimes even three digits. But guessing this was in some way a greeting, I did the same thing by way of reply. He grinned with immense satisfaction. Then his quick roving glance went round again. He made a swift movement, and vanished. The fern fronds he had stood between came swishing together.

I pushed out of the brake after him, and was astonished to find him swinging cheerfully by one lank arm from a rope of creepers that looped down from the foliage overhead. His back was to me.

'Hullo!' said I.

He came down with a twisting jump, and stood facing me. 'I say,' said I, 'where can I get something to eat?'

'Eat!' he said. 'Eat man's food now.' And his eyes went back to the swing of the ropes. 'At the huts.'

'But where are the huts?'

'Oh!'

'I'm new, you know.'

At that he swung round, and set off at a quick walk. All his motions were curiously rapid. 'Come along,' said he. I went with him to see the adventure out. I guessed the huts were some rough shelter, where he and some more of these Beast People lived. I might perhaps find them friendly, find some handle in their minds to take hold of. I did not know yet how far they had forgotten the human heritage I ascribed them.

My ape-like companion trotted along by my side, with his hands hanging down and his jaw thrust forward. I wondered what memory he might have in him. 'How long have you been on this island?' said I.

'How long?' he asked. And, after having the question

repeated, he held up three fingers. The creature was little better than an idiot. I tried to make out what he meant by that, and it seems I bored him. After another question or two, he suddenly left my side and sprang at some fruit that hung from a tree. He pulled down a handful of prickly husks, and went on eating the contents. I noted this with satisfaction, for here, at least, was a hint for feeding. I tried him with some other questions, but his chattering prompt responses were, as often as not, quite at cross-purposes with my question. Some few were appropriate, others quite parrot-like.

I was so intent upon these peculiarities that I scarcely noticed the path we followed. Presently we came to trees, all charred and brown, and so to a bare place covered with a yellow-white incrustation, across which a drifting smoke, pungent in whiffs to nose and eyes, went drifting. On our right, over a shoulder of bare rock, I saw the level blue of the sea. The path coiled down abruptly into a narrow ravine between two tumbled and knotty masses of blackish scoriæ. Into this we plunged.

It was extremely dark, this passage, after the blinding sunlight reflected from the sulphurous ground. Its walls grew steep, and approached one another. Blotches of green and crimson drifted across my eyes. My conductor stopped suddenly. 'Home,' said he, and I stood in a floor of a chasm that was at first absolutely dark to me. I heard some strange noises, and thrust the knuckles of my left hand into my eyes. I became aware of a disagreeable odour like that of a monkey's cage ill-cleaned. Beyond, the rock opened again upon a gradual slope of sunlit greenery, and on either hand the light smote down through a narrow channel into the central gloom.

12

The Sayers of the Law

Then something cold touched my hand. I started violently, and saw close to me a dim pinkish thing, looking more like a flayed child than anything else in the world. The creature had exactly the mild but repulsive features of a sloth, and same low forehead and slow gestures. As the first shock of the change of light passed, I saw about me more distinctly. The little sloth-like creature was standing and staring at me. My conductor had vanished.

The place was a narrow passage between high walls of lava, a crack in its knotted flow, and on either side interwoven heaps of sea-mat, palm fans and reeds leaning against the rock, formed rough and impenetrably dark dens. The winding way up the ravine between these was scarcely three yards wide, and was disfigured by lumps of decaying fruit-pulp and other refuse, which accounted for the disagreeable stench of the place.

The little pink sloth creature was still blinking at me when my Ape Man reappeared at the aperture of the nearest of these dens, and beckoned me in. As he did so a slouching monster wriggled out of one of the places further up this strange street, and stood up in featureless silhouette against the bright green beyond, staring at me. I hesitated – had half a mind to bolt the way I had come – and then, determined to go through with the adventure, gripped my nailed stick about the middle, and crawled into the little evil-smelling lean-to after my conductor.

It was a semicircular space, shaped like the half of a bee-hive, and against the rocky wall that formed the inner side of it was a pile of variegated fruits, cocoa-nuts and others. Some rough vessels and wood stood about the floor, and one on a rough stool. There was no fire. In the darkest corner of the hut sat a shapeless mass of darkness that grunted 'Hey !' as I came in, and my Ape Man stood in the dim light of the doorway and held out a split cocoa-nut to me as I crawled into the other corner and squatted down. I took it and began gnawing it, as serenely as possible, in spite of my tense trepidation, and the nearly intolerable closeness of the den. The little pink sloth creature stood in the aperture of the hut, and something else with a drab face and bright eyes came staring over its shoulder.

'Hey,' came out of the lump of mystery opposite. 'It is a man ! It is a man !' gabbled my conductor – 'a man, a man, a live man, like me.'

'Shut up !' said the voice from the dark, and grunted. I gnawed my cocoa-nut amid an impressive silence. I peered hard into the blackness, but could distinguish nothing. 'It is a man,' the voice repeated. 'He comes to live with us ?' It was a thick voice with something in it, a kind of whistling overtone, that struck me as peculiar, but the English accent was strangely good.

The Ape Man looked at me as though he expected something. I perceived the pause was interrogative. 'He comes to live with you,' I said.

'It is a man. He must learn the Law.'

I began to distinguish now a deeper blackness in the black, a vague outline of a hunched-up figure. Then I noticed the opening of the place was darkened by two more heads. My hand tightened on my stick. The thing in the dark repeated in a louder tone, 'Say the words.' I had missed its last remark. 'Not to go on all-Fours; that is the Law' – it repeated in a kind of sing-song.

I was puzzled. 'Say the words,' said the Ape Man, repeating, and the figures in the doorway echoed this with a threat in the tone of their voices. I realised I had to repeat this idiotic formula. And then began the insanest ceremony. The voice in the dark began intoning a mad litany, line by line, and I and the rest to repeat it. As they did so, they swayed from side to side, and beat their hands upon their knees, and I followed their example. I could have imagined I was already dead and in another world. The dark hut, these grotesque dim figures, just flecked here and there by a glimmer of light, and all of them swaying in unison and chanting : –

'Not to go on all-Fours; *that* is the Law. Are we not Men?'

'Not to suck up Drink; *that* is the Law. Are we not Men?'

'Not to eat Flesh nor Fish; *that* is the Law. Are we not Men?'

'Not to claw Bark of Trees; *that* is the Law. Are we not Men?'

'Not to chase other Men; *that* is the Law. Are we not Men?'

And so from the prohibition of these acts of folly, on to the prohibition of what I thought then were the maddest, most impossible, and most indecent things one could well imagine. A kind of rhythmic fervour fell on all of us; we gabbled and swayed faster and faster, repeating this amazing law. Superficially the contagion of these brute men was upon me, but deep down within me laughter and disgust struggled together. We ran through a long list of prohibitions, and then the chant swung round to a new formula: —

'*His* is the House of Pain.

'*His* is the Hand that makes.

'*His* is the Hand that wounds.

'*His* is the Hand that heals.'

And so on for another long series, mostly quite incomprehensible gibberish to me, about *Him*, whoever he might be. I could have fancied it was a dream, but never before have I heard chanting in a dream.

'*His* is the lightning-flash,' we sang. '*His* is the deep salt sea.'

A horrible fancy came into my head that Moreau, after animalising these men, had infected their dwarfed brains with a kind of deification of himself. However, I was too keenly aware of white teeth and strong claws about me to stop my chanting on that account. '*His* are the stars in the sky.'

At last that song ended. I saw the Ape Man's face shining with perspiration, and my eyes being now accustomed to the darkness, I saw more distinctly the figure in the corner from which the voice came. It was the size of a man, but it seemed covered with a dull grey hair almost like a Skye terrier. What was it? What were they all? Imagine yourself surrounded by all the most horrible cripples and maniacs it is possible to conceive, and you may understand a little of my feelings with these grotesque caricatures of humanity about me.

'He is a five-man, a five-man, a five-man . . . like me,' said the Ape Man.

I held out my hands. The grey creature in the corner leant forward. 'Not to run on all-Fours; that is the Law. Are we not Men?' he said. He put out a strangely distorted talon, and gripped my fingers. The thing was almost like the hoof of a deer produced into claws. I could have yelled with surprise and pain. His face came forward and peered at my nails, came forward into the light of the opening of the hut, and I saw with a quivering disgust that it was like the face of neither man nor beast, but a mere shock of grey hair, with three shadowy overarchings to mark the eyes and mouth.

'He has little nails,' said this grisly creature in his hairy beard. 'It is well.'

He threw my hand down, and instinctively I gripped my stick. 'Eat roots and herbs – it is His will,' said the Ape Man.

'I am the Sayer of the Law,' said the grey figure. 'Here come all that be new, to learn the Law. I sit in the darkness and say the Law.'

'It is even so,' said one of the beasts in the doorway.

'Evil are the punishments of those who break the Law. None escape.'

'None escape,' said the Beast Folk, glancing furtively at each other.

'None, none,' said the Ape Man. 'None escape. See! I did a little thing, a wrong thing, once. I jabbered, jabbered, stopped talking. None could understand. I am burnt, branded in the hand. He is great, he is good!'

'None escape,' said the grey creature in the corner.

'None escape,' said the Beast People, looking askance at one another.

'For every one the want that is bad,' said the grey Sayer of the Law. 'What you will want, we do not know. We shall know. Some want to follow things that move, to watch and slink and wait and spring, to kill and bite, bite deep and rich, sucking the blood . . . It is bad. "Not to chase other Men; that is the Law. *Are we not Men*? Not to eat Flesh nor Fish; that is the Law. *Are we not Men*?"'

'None escape,' said a dappled brute standing in the doorway.

'For every one the want that is bad,' said the grey Sayer of the Law. 'Some want to go tearing with teeth and hands into the roots of things, snuffing into the earth . . . It is bad.'

'None escape,' said the men in the door.

'Some go clawing trees, some go scratching at the graves of the dead; some go fighting with foreheads or feet or claws; some bite suddenly, none giving occasion; some love uncleanness.'

'None escape,' said the Ape Man, scratching his calf.

'None escape,' said the little pink sloth creature.

'Punishment is sharp and sure. Therefore learn the Law. Say the words,' and incontinently he began again the strange litany of the Law, and again I and all these creatures began singing and swaying. My head reeled with this jabbering and the close stench of the place, but I kept on, trusting to find presently some chance of a new development. 'Not to go on all-Fours; that is the Law. *Are we not Men* ?'

We were making such a noise that I noticed nothing of a tumult outside, until some one, who, I think, was one of the two Swine Men I had seen, thrust his head over the little pink sloth creature and shouted something excitedly, something that I did not catch. Incontinently those at the opening of the hut vanished, my Ape Man rushed out, the thing that had sat in the dark followed him – I only observed it was big and clumsy, and covered with silvery hair, – and I was left alone.

Then before I reached the aperture I heard the yelp of a staghound.

In another moment I was standing outside the hovel, my chair-rail in my hand, every muscle of me quivering. Before me were the clumsy backs of perhaps a score of these Beast People, their misshapen heads half-hidden by their shoulder-blades. They were gesticulating excitedly. Other half-animal faces glared interrogation out of the hovels. Looking in the direction in which they faced I saw coming through the haze under the trees beyond the end of the passage of dens the dark figure and awful white face of Moreau. He was holding the leaping staghound back, and close behind him came Montgomery, revolver in hand.

For a moment I stood horror-struck.

I turned and saw the passages behind me blocked by another heavy brute with a huge grey face and twinkling little eyes, advancing towards me. I looked round and saw to the right of me, and half a dozen yards in front of me, a narrow gap in the wall of rock through which a ray of light slanted into the shadows. 'Stop!' cried Moreau, as I strode towards this, and then, 'Hold him!' At that, first one face turned towards me, and then others. Their bestial minds were happily slow.

I dashed my shoulder into a clumsy monster who was turning to see what Moreau meant, and flung him forward into another. I felt his hands fly round, clutching at me and missing me. The little pink sloth creature dashed at me and I cut it over, gashed down its ugly face with the nail in my stick, and in another minute I was scrambling up a steep side pathway, a kind of sloping chimney out of the ravine. I heard a howl behind me, and cries of 'Catch him!' 'Hold him!' and the grey-faced creature appeared behind me and jammed his huge bulk into the cleft. 'Go on, go on!' they howled. I clambered up the narrow cleft in the rock, and came out upon the sulphur on the westward side of the village of the Beast Men.

That gap was altogether fortunate for me, for the narrow way slanting obliquely upward must have impeded the nearer pursuers. I ran over the white space and down a steep slope through a scattered growth of trees, and came to a low-lying stretch of tall reeds. Through this I pushed into a dark thick undergrowth that was black and succulent under foot. As I plunged into the reeds my foremost pursuers emerged from the gap. I broke my way through this undergrowth for some minutes. The air behind me and about me was soon full of threatening cries. I heard the tumult of my pursuers in the gap up the shore, then the crashing of the reeds, and every now and then the crackling crash of a branch. Some of the creatures roared like excited beasts of prey. I heard Moreau and Montgomery shouting in the same direction. I turned sharply to the right. It seemed to me even then that I heard Montgomery shouting for me to run for my life.

Presently the ground gave, rich and oozy, under my feet; but I was desperate, and went headlong into it, struggled through knee-deep, and so came to a winding path among tall canes. The noise of my pursuers passed away to my left. In one place three strange pink hopping animals, about the size of cats, bolted before my footsteps. This pathway ran uphill, across another open space covered with white incrustation, and plunged into a cane brake again.

Then suddenly it turned parallel with the edge of a steep walled gap which came without warning like the haha of an English park – turned with unexpected abruptness. I was still running with all my might, and I never saw this drop until I was flying headlong through the air.

I fell on my forearms and head, among thorns, and rose with a torn ear and bleeding face. I had fallen into a precipitous ravine, rocky and thorny, full of a hazy mist that drifted about me in wisps, and with a narrow streamlet, from which this mist came, meandering down the centre. I was astonished at this thin fog in the full blaze of daylight, but I had no time to stand wondering then. I turned to my right down stream, hoping to come to the sea in that direction, and so have my way open to drown myself. It was only later I found that I had dropped my nailed stick in my fall.

Presently the ravine grew narrower for a space, and carelessly I stepped into the stream. I jumped out again pretty quickly, for the water was almost boiling. I noticed too there was a thin sulphurous scum drifting upon its coiling water. Almost immediately came a turn in the ravine and the indistinct blue horizon. The nearer sea was flashing the sun from a myriad facets. I saw my death before me. But I was hot and panting, with the warm blood oozing out on my face and running pleasantly through my veins. I felt more than a touch of exultation, too, at having distanced my pursuers. It was not in me then to go out and drown myself. I stared back the way I had come.

I listened. Save for the hum of the gnats and the chirp of some small insects that hopped among the thorns, the air was absolutely still. Then came the yelp of a dog, very faint, and a chattering and gibbering, the snap of a whip and voices. They grew louder, then fainter again. The noise receded up the stream and faded away. For a while the chase was over.

But I knew now how much hope of help for me lay in the Beast People.

13

A Parley

I turned again and went on down towards the sea. I found the hot stream broadened out to a shallow weedy sand, in which an abundance of crabs, and long-bodied, many-legged creatures started from my footfall. I walked to the very edge of the salt water, and then I felt I was safe. I turned and stared – arms akimbo – at the thick green behind me, into which the steamy ravine cut like a smoking gash. But as I say, I was too full of excitement, and – a true saying, though those who have never known danger may doubt it – too desperate to die.

Then it came into my head that there was one chance before me yet. While Moreau and Montgomery and their bestial rabble chased me through the island, might I not go round the beach until I came to their enclosure? – make a flank march upon them, in fact, and then with a rock lugged out of their loosely built wall perhaps, smash in the lock of the smaller door and see what I could find – knife, pistol, or what not – to fight them with when they returned? It was at any rate a chance of getting a price for my life.

So I turned to the westward and walked along by the water's edge. The setting sun flashed his blinding heat into my eyes. The slight Pacific tide was running in with a gentle ripple.

Presently the shore fell away southward and the sun came round upon my right hand. Then suddenly, far in front of me, I saw first one and then several figures emerging from the bushes, – Moreau with his grey staghound, then Montgomery, and two others. At that I stopped.

They saw me and began gesticulating and advancing. I stood watching them approach. The two Beast Men came running forward to cut me off from the undergrowth inland. Montgomery came running also, but straight towards me. Moreau followed slower with the dog.

At last I roused myself from inaction, and turning seaward walked straight into the water. The water was very shallow at first. I was thirty yards out before the waves reached to my waist. Dimly I could see the inter-tidal creatures darting away from my feet.

'What are you doing, man?' cried Montgomery.

I turned, standing waist-deep, and stared at them.

Montgomery stood panting at the margin of the water. His face was bright red with exertion, his long flazen hair blown about his head, and his dropping nether lip showed his irregular teeth. Moreau was just coming up, his face pale and firm, and the dog at his hand barked at me. Both men had heavy whips. Further up the beach stared the Beast Men.

'What am I doing? – I am going to drown myself,' said I.

Montgomery and Moreau looked at one another. 'Why?' asked Moreau.

'Because that is better than being tortured by you.'

'I told you so,' said Montgomery, and Moreau said something in a low tone.

'What makes you think I shall torture you?' asked Moreau.

'What I saw,' I said. 'And those – yonder.'

'Hush!' said Moreau, and held up his hand.

'I will not,' said I; 'they were men: what are they now? I at least will not be like them.' I looked past my interlocutors. Up the beach were M'ling, Montgomery's attendant, and one of the white swathed brutes from the boat. Further up, in the shadow of the trees, I saw my little Ape Man, and behind him some other dim figures.

'Who are these creatures?' said I, pointing to them, and raising my voice more and more that it might reach them. 'They were men – men like yourselves, whom you have infected with some bestial taint, men whom you have enslaved, and whom you still fear. – You who listen,' I cried, pointing now to Moreau, and shouting past him to the Beast Men, 'You who listen! Do you not see these men still fear you, go in dread of you? Why then do you fear them? You are many –'

'For God's sake,' cried Montgomery, 'stop that, Prendick!'

'Prendick!' cried Moreau.

They both shouted together as if to drown my voice. And behind them lowered the staring faces of the Beast Men, wondering, their deformed hands hanging down, their shoulders hunched up. They seemed, as I fancied then, to be trying to understand me, to remember something of their human past.

I went on shouting, I scarcely remember what. That Moreau and Montgomery could be killed; that they were not to be feared: that was the burthen of what I put into the heads of the Beast People to my own ultimate undoing. I saw the green-eyed man in the dark rags, who had met me on the evening of my arrival, come out from among the trees, and others followed him to hear me better.

At last for want of breath I paused.

'Listen to me for a moment,' said the steady voice of Moreau, 'and then say what you will.'

'Well?' said I.

He coughed, thought, then shouted: 'Latin, Prendick! Bad Latin! Schoolboy Latin! But try and understand. *Hi non sunt homines, sunt animalia qui nos habemus* ... vivisected. A humanising process. I will explain. Come ashore.'

I laughed. 'A pretty story,' said I. 'They talk, build houses, cook. They were men. It's likely I'll come ashore.'

'The water just beyond where you stand is deep ... and full of sharks.'

'That's my way,' said I. 'Short and sharp. Presently.'

'Wait a minute.' He took something out of his pocket that flashed back the sun, and dropped the object at his feet. 'That's a loaded revolver,' said he. 'Montgomery here will do the same. Now we are going up the beach until you are satisfied the distance is safe. Then come and take the revolvers.'

'Not I. You have a third between you.'

'I want you to think over things, Prendick. In the first place, I never asked you to come upon this island. In the next, we had you drugged last night, had we wanted to work you any mischief; and in the next, now your first panic is over, and you can think a little – is Montgomery here quite up to the character you give him ? We have chased you for your good. Because this island is full of . . . inimical phenomena. Why should we want to shoot you when you have just offered to drown yourself ?'

'Why did you set . . . your people on to me when I was in the hut ?'

'We felt sure of catching you and bringing you out of danger. Afterwards we drew away from the scent – for your good.'

I mused. It seemed just possible. Then I remembered something again.

'But I saw,' said I, 'in the enclosure – '

'That was the puma.'

'Look here, Prendick,' said Montgomery. 'You're a silly ass. Come out of the water and take these revolvers, and talk. We can't do anything more than we could do now.'

I will confess that then, and indeed always, I distrusted and dreaded Moreau. But Montgomery was a man I felt I understood.

'Go up the beach,' said I, after thinking, and added, 'holding your hands up.'

'Can't do that,' said Montgomery, with an explanatory nod over his shoulder. 'Undignified.'

'Go up to the trees, then,' said I, 'as you please.'

'It's a damned silly ceremony,' said Montgomery.

Both turned and faced the six or seven grotesque creatures, who stood there in the sunlight, solid, casting shadows, moving, and yet so incredibly unreal. Montgomery cracked his whip at them, and forthwith they all turned and fled helter-skelter into the trees. And when Montgomery and Moreau were at a distance I judged sufficient, I waded ashore, and picked up and examined the revolvers. To satisfy myself against the subtlest trickery I discharged one at a rounded lump of lava, and had the satisfaction of seeing the stone pulverised and the beach splashed with lead.

Still I hesitated for a moment.

'I'll take the risk,' said I, at last, and with a revolver in each hand I walked up the beach towards them.

'That's better,' said Moreau, without affectation. 'As it is, you have wasted the best part of my day with your confounded imagination.'

And with a touch of contempt that humiliated me he and Montgomery turned and went on in silence before me.

The knot of Beast Men, still wondering, stood back among the trees. I passed them as serenely as possible. One started to follow me, but retreated again when Montgomery cracked his whip. The rest stood silent – watching. They may once have been animals. But I never before saw an animal trying to think.

14

Doctor Moreau explains

'And now, Prendick, I will explain,' said Doctor Moreau, so soon as we had eaten and drunk. 'I must confess you are the most dictatorial guest I ever entertained. I warn you that this is the last I do to oblige you. The next thing you threaten to commit suicide about I shan't do – even at some personal inconvenience.'

He sat in my deck chair, a cigar half consumed in his white dexterous-looking fingers. The light of the swinging lamp fell on his white hair; he stared through the little window out at the starlight. I sat as far away from him as possible, the table between us and the revolvers to hand. Montgomery was not present. I did not care to be with the two of them in such a little room.

'You admit that vivisected human being, as you called it, is, after all, only the puma?' said Moreau. He had made me visit that horror in the inner room to assure myself of its inhumanity.

'It is the puma,' I said, 'still alive, but so cut and mutilated as I pray I may never see living flesh again. Of all vile – '

'Never mind that,' said Moreau. 'At least spare me those youthful horrors. Montgomery used to be just the same. You admit it is the puma. Now be quiet while I reel off my physiological lecture to you.' And forthwith, beginning in the tone of a man supremely bored, but presently warming a little, he explained his work to me. He was very simple and convincing. Now and then there was a touch of sarcasm in his voice. Presently I found myself hot with shame at our mutual positions.

The creatures I had seen were not men, had never been men. They were animals – humanised animals – triumphs of vivisection.

'You forget all that a skilled vivisector can do with living things,' said Moreau. 'For my own part I'm puzzled why the things I have done here have not been done before. Small efforts of course have been made – amputation, tongue-cutting, excisions. Of course you know a squint may be induced or cured by surgery? Then in the case of excisions you have all kinds of secondary changes, pigmentary disturbances, modifications of the passions, alterations in the secretion of fatty tissue. I have no doubt you have heard of these things?'

'Of course,' said I. 'But these foul creatures of yours – '

'All in good time,' said he, waving his hand at me; 'I am only beginning. Those are trivial cases of alteration. Surgery can do better things than that. There is building up as well as breaking down and changing. You have heard, perhaps, of a common surgical operation resorted to in cases where the nose has been destroyed. A flap of skin is cut from the forehead, turned down on the nose, and heals in the new position. This is a kind of grafting in a new position of part of an animal upon itself. Grafting of freshly obtained material from another animal is also possible, – the case of teeth, for example. The grafting of skin and bone is done to facilitate healing. The surgeon places in the middle of the wound pieces of skin snipped from another animal, or fragments of bone from a victim freshly killed. Hunter's cockspur – possibly you have heard of that – flourished on the bull's neck. And the rhinoceros rats of the Algerian zouaves are also to be thought of, – monsters manufactured by transferring a slip from the tail of an ordinary rat to its snout, and allowing it to heal in that position.'

'Monsters manufactured!' said I. 'Then you mean to tell me – '

'Yes. These creatures you have seen are animals carven and wrought into new shapes. To that – to the study of the plasticity of living forms – my life has been devoted. I have studied for years, gaining in knowledge as I go. I see you look horrified, and yet I am telling you nothing new. It all lay in the surface of practical anatomy years ago, but no one had the temerity to touch it. It's not simply the outward form of an animal I can change. The physiology, the chemical rhythm of the creature, may also be made to undergo an enduring modification, of which vaccination and other methods of inoculation with living or dead matter are examples that will, no doubt, be familiar to you. A similar operation is the transfusion of blood, with which subject indeed I began. These are all familiar cases. Less so, and probably far more extensive, were the operations of those mediæval practitioners who made dwarfs and beggar cripples and show-monsters; some vestiges of whose art still remain in the preliminary manipulation of the young mountebank or contortionist. Victor Hugo gives an account of them in *L'Homme qui Rit* ... But perhaps my meaning grows plain now. You begin to see that it is a possible thing to transplant tissue from one part of an animal to another, or from one animal to another, to alter its chemical reactions and methods of growth, to modify the articulations of its limbs, and indeed to change it in its most intimate structure?

'And yet this extraordinary branch of knowledge has never been sought as an end, and systematically, by modern investigatores, until I took it up! Some such things have been hit upon in the last resort of surgery; most of the kindred evidence that will recur to your mind has been demonstrated, as it were, by accident – by tyrants, by criminals, by the breeders of horses and dogs, by all kinds of untrained clumsy-handed men working for their own immediate ends. I was the first man to take up this question armed with antiseptic surgery, and with a really scientific knowledge of the laws of growth.

'Yet one would imagine it must have been practised in secret before. Such creatures as the Siamese Twins ... And in the vaults of the Inquisition. No doubt their chief aim was artistic torture, but some, at least, of the inquisitors must have had a touch of scientific curiosity ...'

'But,' said I. 'These things – these animals *talk* !'

He said that was so, and proceeded to point out that the possibilities of vivisection do not stop at a mere physical metamorphosis. A pig may be educated. The mental structure is even less determinate than the bodily. In our growing science of hypnotism we find the promise of a possibility of replacing old inherent instincts by new suggestions, grafting upon or replacing the inherited fixed ideas. Very much, indeed, of what we call moral education is such an artificial modification and perversion of instinct; pugnacity is trained into courageous self-sacrifice, and suppressed sexuality into religious emotion. And the great difference between man and monkey is in the larynx, he said, in the incapacity to frame delicately different sound-symbols by which thought could be sustained. In this I failed to agree with him, but with a certain incivility he declined to notice my objection. He repeated that the thing was so, and continued his account of his work.

But I asked him why he had taken the human form as a model. There seemed to me then, and there still seems to me now, a strange wickedness in that choice.

He confessed that he had chosen that form by chance. 'I might just as well have worked to form sheep into llamas, and llamas into sheep. I suppose there is something in the human form that appeals to the artistic turn of mind more powerfully than any animal shape can. But I've not confined myself to man-making. Once or twice . . .' He was silent, for a minute perhaps. 'These years! How they have slipped by! And here I have wasted a day saving your life, and am now wasting an hour explaining myself!'

'But,' said I, 'I still do not understand. Where is your justification for inflicting all this pain? The only thing that could excuse vivisection to me would be some application – '

'Precisely,' said he. 'But you see I am differently constituted. We are on different platforms. You are a materialist.'

'I am *not* a materialist,' I began hotly.

'In my view – in my view. For it is just this question of pain that parts us. So long as visible or audible pain turns you sick, so long as your own pains drive you, so long as pain underlies your propositions about sin, so long, I tell you, you are an animal, thinking a little less obscurely what an animal feels. This pain – '

I gave an impatient shrug at such sophistry.

'Oh! but it is such a little thing. A mind truly opened to what science has to teach must see that it is a little thing. It may be that, save in this little planet, this speck of cosmic dust, invisible long before the nearest star could be attained – it may be, I say, that nowhere else does this thing called pain occur. But the laws we feel our way towards ... Why, even on this earth, even among living things, what pain is there ?'

He drew a little penknife as he spoke from his pocket, opened the smaller blade and moved his chair so that I could see his thigh. Then, choosing the place deliberately, he drove the blade into his leg and withdrew it.

'No doubt you have seen that before. It does not hurt a pin-prick. But what does it show ? The capacity for pain is not needed in the muscle, and it is not placed there; it is but little needed in the skin, and only here and there over the thigh is a spot capable of feeling pain. Pain is simply our intrinsic medical adviser to warn and stimulate us. All living flesh is not painful, nor is all nerve, nor even all sensory nerve. There's no taint of pain, real pain, in the sensations of the optic nerve. If you wound the optic nerve you merely see flashes of light, just as disease of the auditory nerve merely means a humming in our ears. Plants do not feel pain; the lower animals – it's possible that such animals as the starfish and crayfish do not feel pain. Then with men, the more intelligent they become the more intelligently they will see after their own welfare, and the less they will need the goad to keep them out of danger. I never yet heard of a useless thing that was not ground out of existence by evolution sooner or later. Did you ? And pain gets needless.

'Then I am a religious man, Prendick, as every sane man must be. It may be I fancy I have seen more of the ways of this world's Maker than you – for I have sought his laws, in *my* way, all my life, while you, I understand, have been collecting butterflies. And I tell you, pleasure and pain have nothing to do with heaven or hell. Pleasure and pain – Bah ! What is your theologian's ecstasy but Mahomet's houri in the dark ? This store men and women set on pleasure and pain, Prendick, is the mark of the beast upon them, the mark of the beast from which they came. Pain ! Pain and pleasure – they are for us, only so long as we wriggle in the dust ...

'You see, I went on with this research just the way it led me. That is the only way I ever heard of research going. I asked a question, devised some method of getting an answer, and got –

a fresh question. Was this possible, or that possible? You cannot imagine what this means to an investigator, what an intellectual passion grows upon him. You cannot imagine the strange colourless delight of these intellectual desires. The thing before you is no longer an animal, a fellow-creature, but a problem. Sympathetic pain – all I know of it I remember as a thing I used to suffer from years ago. I wanted – it was the only thing I wanted – to find out the extreme limit of plasticity in a living shape.'

'But,' said I, 'the thing is an abomination – '

'To this day I have never troubled about the ethics of the matter. The study of Nature makes a man at last as remorseless as Nature. I have gone on, not heeding anything but the question I was pursuing, and the material has ... dripped into the huts yonder ... It is nearly eleven years since we came here, I and Montgomery and six Kanakas. I remember the green stillness of the island and the empty ocean about us as though it was yesterday. The place seemed waiting for me.

'The stores were landed and the house was built. The Kanakas founded some huts near the ravine. I went to work here upon what I had brought with me. There were some disagreeable things happened at first. I began with a sheep, and killed it after a day and a half by a slip of the scalpel; I took another sheep and made a thing of pain and fear, and left it bound up to heal. It looked quite human to me when I had finished it, but when I went to it I was discontented with it; it remembered me, and was terrified beyond imagination, and it had no more than the wits of a sheep. The more I looked at it the clumsier it seemed, until at last I put the monster out of its misery. These animals without courage, these fear-haunted pain-driven things, without a spark of pugnacious energy to face torment – they are no good for man-making.

'Then I took a gorilla I had, and upon that, working with infinite care, and mastering difficulty after difficulty, I made my first man. All the week, night and day, I moulded him. With him it was chiefly the brain that needed moulding; much had to be added, much changed. I thought him a fair specimen of the negroid type when I had done him, and he lay, bandaged, bound, and motionless before me. It was only when his life was assured that I left him, and came into the room again and found Montgomery much as you are. He had heard some of the cries as the thing grew human, cries like those that disturbed *you* so. I didn't take him completely into my confidence at first. And the Kanakas, too, had realised something of it. They were scared out of their wits by the sight of me. I got Montgomery over to me – in a way, but I and he had the hardest job to prevent the Kanakas deserting. Finally they did, and so we lost the yacht. I spent many days educating the brute – altogether I had him for three or four months. I taught him the rudiments of English, gave him ideas of counting, even made the thing read the alphabet. But at that he was slow – though I've met with idiots slower. He began with a clean sheet, mentally; had no memories left in his mind of what he had been. When his scars were quite healed, and he was no longer anything but painful and stiff, and able to converse a little, I took him yonder and introduced him to the Kanakas as an interesting stowaway.

'They were horribly afraid of him at first, somehow – which offended me rather, for I was conceited about him, – but his ways seemed so mild, and he was so abject, that after a time they received him and took his education in hand. He was quick to learn, very imitative and adaptive, and built himself a hovel rather better, it seemed to me, than their own shanties. There was one among the boys, a bit of a missionary, and he taught the thing to read, or at least to pick out letters, and gave him some rudimentary ideas of morality, but it seems the beast's habits were not all that is desirable.

'I rested from work for some days, and was in a mind to write an account of the whole affair to wake up English physiology. Then I came upon the creature squatting up in a tree gibbering at two of the Kanakas who had been teasing him. I threatened him, told him the inhumanity of such a proceeding, aroused his sense of shame, and came here resolved to do better before I took my work back to England. I have been doing better; but somehow the things drift back again, the stubborn beast flesh grows, day by day, back again . . . I mean to do better things still. I mean to conquer that. This puma . . .

'But that's the story. All the Kanaka boys are dead now. One fell overboard of the launch, and one died of a wounded heel that he poisoned in some way with plant-juice. Three went away in the yacht, and I suppose, and hope, were drowned. The other one . . . was killed. Well – I have replaced them. Montgomery went on much as you are disposed to do at first, and then . . .'

'What became of the other one ?' said I sharply, – 'the other Kanaka who was killed ?'

'The fact is, after I had made a number of human creatures I made a thing – ' He hesitated.

'Yes ?' said I.

'It was killed.'

'I don't understand,' said I ; 'do you mean to say . . .'

'It killed the Kanaka – yes. It killed several other things that it caught. We chased it for a couple of days. It only got loose by accident – I never meant it to get away. It wasn't finished. It was purely an experiment. It was a limbless thing with a horrible face that writhed along the ground in a serpentine fashion. It was immensely strong and in infuriating pain, and it travelled in a rollicking way like a porpoise swimming. It lurked in the woods for some days, doing mischief to all it came across, until we hunted it, and then it wriggled into the northern part of the island, and we divided the party to close in upon it. Montgomery insisted upon coming with me. The man had a rifle, and when his body was found one of the barrels was curved into the shape of an S, and very nearly bitten through. . . . Montgomery shot the thing . . . After that I stuck to the ideal of humanity – except for little things.'

He became silent. I sat in silence watching his face.

'So for twenty years altogether – counting nine years in England – I have been going on, and there is still something in everything I do that defeats me, makes me dissatisfied, challenges me to further effort. Sometimes I rise above my level, sometimes I fall below it, but always I fall short of the things I dream. The human shape I can get now, almost with ease, so that it is lithe and graceful, or thick and strong ; but often there is trouble with the hands and claws – painful things that I dare not shape too freely. But it is in the subtle grafting and re-shaping one must needs do to the brain that my trouble lies. The intelligence is often oddly low, with unaccountable blank ends, unexpected gaps. And least satisfactory of all is something that I cannot touch, somewhere – I cannot determine where – in the seat of the emotions. Cravings, instincts, desires that harm humanity, a strange hidden reservoir to burst suddenly and inundate the whole being of the creature with anger, hate, or fear. These creatures of mine seemed strange and uncanny to you as soon as you began to observe them, but to me, just after I make them, they seem to be indisputable human beings. It's afterwards as I observe them that the persuasion fades. First one animal trait, then another, creeps to the surface and stares out at me . . . But I will conquer yet. Each time I dip a living creature into the bath of burning pain, I say, This time I will burn out all the animal, this time I will make a rational creature of my own. After all, what is ten years? Man has been a hundred thousand in the making.'

He thought darkly. 'But I am drawing near the fastness. This puma of mine . . .'

After a silence : 'And they revert. As soon as my hand is taken from them the beast begins to creep back, begins to assert itself again . . .'

Another long silence.

'Then you take the things you make into those dens ?' said I.

'They go. I turn them out when I begin to feel the beast in them, and presently they wander there. They all dread this house and me. There is a kind of travesty of humanity over there. Montgomery knows about it, for he interferes in their affairs. He has trained one or two of them to our service. He's ashamed of it, but I believe he half-likes some of these beasts. It's his business, not mine. They only sicken me with a sense of failure. I take no interest in them. I fancy they follow in the lines the Kanaka missionary marked out, and have a kind of mockery of a rational life – poor beasts ! There's something they call the Law. Sing hymns about "all thine." They build themselves their dens, gather fruit and pull herbs – marry even. But I can see through it all, see into their very souls, and see there nothing but the souls of beasts, beasts that perish – anger, and the lusts to live and gratify themselves ... Yet they're odd. Complex, like everything else alive. There is a kind of upward striving in them, part vanity, part waste sexual emotion, part waste curiosity. It only mocks me ... I have some hope of that puma; I have worked hard at her head and brain ...

'And now,' said he, standing up after a long gap of silence, during which we had each pursued our own thoughts; 'what do you think? Are you in fear of me still?'

I looked at him, and saw but a white-faced white-haired man, with calm eyes. Save for his serenity, the touch almost of beauty that resulted from his set tranquillity, and from his magnificent build, he might have passed muster among a hundred other comfortable old gentlemen. Then I shivered. By way of answer to his second question, I handed him a revolver with either hand.

'Keep them,' he said, and snatched at a yawn. He stood up, stared at me for a moment, and smiled. 'You have had two eventful days,' said he. 'I should advise some sleep. I'm glad it's all clear. Goodnight.'

He thought me over for a moment, then went out by the inner door. I immediately turned the key in the outer one.

I sat down again, sat for a time in a kind of stagnant mood, so weary, emotionally, mentally, and physically, that I could not think beyond the point at which he had left me. The black window stared at me like an eye. At last with an effort I put out the lamp, and got into the hammock. Very soon I was asleep.

15

Concerning the Beast Folk

I woke early. Moreau's explanation stood before my mind, clear and definite, from the moment of my awakening. I got out of the hammock and went to the door to assure myself that the key was turned. Then I tried the window-bar, and found it firmly fixed. That these man-like creatures were in truth only bestial monsters, mere grotesque travesties of men, filled me with a vague uncertainty of their possibilities that was far worse than any definite fear. A tapping came at the door, and I heard the glutinous accents of M'ling speaking. I pocketed one of the revolvers (keeping one hand upon it), and opened to him.

'Good-morning, sair,' he said, bringing in, in addition to the customary herb breakfast, an ill-cooked rabbit. Montgomery followed him. His roving eye caught the position of my arm, and he smiled askew.

The puma was resting to heal that day; but Moreau, who was singularly solitary in his habits, did not join us. I talked with Montgomery to clear my ideas of the way in which the Beast Folk lived. In particular, I was urgent to know how these inhuman monsters were kept from falling upon Moreau and Montgomery, and from rending one another.

He explained to me that the comparative safety of Moreau and himself was due to the limited mental scope of these monsters. In spite of their increased intelligence, and the tendency of their animal instincts to re-awaken, they had certain Fixed Ideas implanted by Moreau in their minds, which absolutely bounded their imaginations. They were really hypnotised, had been told certain things were impossible, and certain things were not to be done, and these prohibitions were woven into the texture of their minds beyond any possibility of disobedience or dispute. Certain matters, however, in which old instinct was at war with Moreau's convenience, were in a less stable condition. A series of propositions called the Law – I had already heard them recited – battled in their minds with the deep-seated, ever rebellious cravings of their animal natures. This Law they were ever repeating, I found, and – ever breaking. Both Montgomery and Moreau displayed particular solicitude to keep them ignorant of the taste of blood. They feared the inevitable suggestions of that flavour.

Montgomery told me that the Law, especially among the feline Beast People, became oddly weakened about nightfall; that then the animal was at its strongest; a spirit of adventure sprang up in them at the dusk; they would dare things they never seemed to dream about by day. To that I owed my stalking by the Leopard Man on the night of my arrival. But during these earlier days of my stay they broke the Law only furtively, and after dark; in the daylight there was a general atmosphere of respect for its multifarious prohibitions.

And here perhaps I may give a few general facts about the island and the Beast People. The island, which was of irregular outline, and lay low upon the wide sea, had a total area, I suppose, of seven or eight square miles.[1] It was volcanic in origin, and was now fringed on three sides by coral reefs. Some fumarolles to the northward, and a hot spring, were the only vestiges of the forces that had long since originated it. Now and then a faint quiver of earthquake would be sensible, and sometimes the ascent of the spire of smoke would be rendered tumultuous by gusts of steam. But that was all. The population of the island, Montgomery informed me, now numbered rather more than sixty of these strange creations of Moreau's art, not counting the smaller monstrosities which lived in the undergrowth and were without human form. Altogether, he had made nearly a hundred and twenty, but many had died; and others, like the writhing Footless Thing of which he had told me, had come by violent ends. In answer to my question, Montgomery said that they actually bore off-spring, but that these generally died. There was no evidence of the inheritance of the acquired

---

[1] This description corresponds in every respect to Noble's Isle. – C.E.P.

human characteristics. When they lived, Moreau took them and stamped the human form upon them. The females were less numerous than the males, and liable to much furtive persecution in spite of the monogamy the Law enjoined.

It would be impossible for me to describe these Beast People in detail – my eye has had no training in details – and unhappily I cannot sketch. Most striking perhaps in their general appearance was the disproportion between the legs of these creatures and the length of their bodies; and yet – so relative is our idea of grace – my eye became habituated to their forms, and at last I even fell in with their persuasion that my own long thighs were ungainly. Another point was the forward carriage of the head, and the clumsy and inhuman curvature of the spine. Even the Ape Man lacked that inward sinuous curve of the back that makes the human figure so graceful. Most had their shoulders hunched clumsily, and their short forearms hung weakly at their sides. Few of them were conspicuously hairy – at least, until the end of my time upon the island.

The next most obvious deformity was in their faces, almost all of which were prognathous, malformed about the ears, with large and protuberant noses, very furry or very bristly hair, and often strangely coloured or strangely placed eyes. None could laugh, though the Ape Man had a chattering titter. Beyond these general characters their heads had little in common; each preserved the quality of its particular species: the human mark distorted but did not hide the leopard, the ox, or the sow, or other animal or animals, from which the creature had been moulded. The voices, too, varied exceedingly. The hands were always malformed; and though some surprised me by their unexpected humanity, almost all were deficient in the number of the digits, clumsy about the finger-nails, and lacking any tactile sensibility.

The two most formidable animal-men were my Leopard Man and a creature made of Hyæna and Swine. Larger than these were the three bull creatures who pulled in the boat. Then came the Silvery Hairy Man, who was also the Sayer of the Law, M'ling, and a satyr-like creature of Ape and Goat. There were three Swine Men and a Swine Woman, a Mare-Rhinoceros creature, and several other females whose sources I did not ascertain. There were several Wolf creatures, a Bear-Bull, and a Saint Bernard Dog Man. I have already described the Ape Man, and there was a particularly hateful (and evil-smelling) old woman made of Vixen and Bear, whom I hated from the beginning. She was said to be a passionate votary of the Law. Smaller creatures were certain dappled youths and my little sloth creature. But enough of this catalogue !

At first I had a shivering horror of the brutes, felt all too keenly that they were still brutes, but insensibly I became a little habituated to the idea of them, and, moreover I was affected by Montgomery's attitude towards them. He had been with them so long that he had come to regard them as almost normal human beings – his London days seemed a glorious impossible past to him. Only once in a year or so did he go to Arica to deal with Moreau's agent, a trader in animals there. He hardly met the finest type of mankind in that seafaring village of Spanish mongrels. The man aboard ship, he told me, seemed at first just as strange to him as the Beast Men seemed to me, – unnaturally long in the leg, flat in the face, prominent in the forehead, suspicious, dangerous, and cold-hearted. In fact, he did not like men. His heart had warmed to me, he thought, because he had saved my life.

I fancied even then that he had a sneaking kindness for some of these metamorphosed brutes, a vicious sympathy with some of their ways, but that he attempted to veil from me at first.

M'ling, the black-faced man, his attendant, the first of the Beast Folk I had encountered, did not live with the others across the island, but in a small kennel at the back of the enclosure. The creature was scarcely so intelligent as the Ape Man, but far more docile, and the most human-looking of all the Beast Folk, and Montgomery had trained it to prepare food, and indeed to discharge all the trivial domestic offices that were required. It was a complex trophy of Moreau's horrible skill, a bear, tainted with dog and ox, and one of the most elaborately made of all his creatures. It treated Montgomery with a strange tenderness and devotion ; sometimes he would notice it, pat it, call it half-mocking, half-jocular names, and so make it caper with extraordinary delight; sometimes he would ill-treat it, especially after he had been at the whisky, kicking it, beating it, pelting it with stones or lighted fuses. But whether he treated it well or ill, it loved nothing so much as to be near him.

I say I became habituated to the Beast People, that a thousand things that had seemed unnatural and repulsive speedily became natural and ordinary to me. I suppose everything in existence takes its colour from the average hue of our surroundings: Montgomery and Moreau were too peculiar and individual to keep my general impressions of humanity well defined. I would see one of the clumsy bovine creatures who worked the launch treading heavily through the undergrowth, and find myself asking, trying hard to recall, how he differed from some really human yokel trudging home from his mechanical labours; or I would meet the Fox-Bear Woman's vulpine shifty face, strangely human in its speculative cunning, and even imagine I had met it before in some city byway.

Yet every now and then the beast would flash out upon me beyond doubt or denial. An ugly-looking man, a hunchbacked human savage to all appearance, squatting in the aperture of one of the dens, would stretch his arms and yawn, showing with startling suddenness scissor-edged incisors and sabre-like canines, keen and brilliant as knives. Or in some narrow pathway, glancing with a transitory daring into the eyes of some lithe white-swathed female figure, I would suddenly see (with a spasmodic revulsion) that they had slit-like pupils, or, glancing down, note the curving nail with which she held her shapeless wrap about her. It is a curious thing, by the by, for which I am quite unable to account, that these weird creatures – the females I mean – had in the earlier days of my stay an instinctive sense of their own repulsive clumsiness, and displayed, in consequence, a more than human regard for the decencies and decorum of external costume.

16

How the Beast Folk Tasted Blood

But my inexperience as a writer betrays me, and I wander from the thread of my story. After I had breakfasted with Montgomery he took me across the island to see the fumarolle and the source of the hot spring, into whose scalding waters I had blundered on the previous day. Both of us carried whips and loaded revolvers. While going through a leafy jungle on our road thither we heard a rabbit squealing. We stopped and listened, but we heard no more, and presently we went on our way, and the incident dropped out of our minds. Montgomery called my attention to certain little pink animals with long hind-legs, that went leaping through the undergrowth. He told me they were creatures made of the offspring of the Beast People, that Moreau had invented. He had fancied they might serve for meat, but a rabbit-like habit of devouring their young had defeated this intention. I had already encountered some of these creatures, once during my moonlight flight from the Leopard Man, and once during my pursuit by Moreau on the previous day. By chance, one hopping to avoid us leapt into the hole caused by the uprooting of a wind-blown tree. Before it could extricate itself we managed to catch it. It spat like a cat, scratched and kicked vigorously with its hind-legs, and made an attempt to bite, but its teeth were too feeble to inflict more than a painless pinch. It seemed to me rather a pretty little creature, and as Montgomery stated that it never destroyed the turf by burrowing, and was very cleanly in its habits, I should imagine it might prove a convenient substitute for the common rabbit in gentlemen's parks.

We also saw on our way the trunk of a tree barked in long strips and splintered deeply. Montgomery called my attention to this. 'Not to claw Bark of Trees; *that* is the Law,' he said.

'Much some of them care for it!' It was after this, I think, that we met the Satyr and the Ape Man. The Satyr was a gleam of classical memory on the part of Moreau, his face ovine in expression – like the coarser Hebrew type, – his voice a harsh bleat, his nether extremities Satanic. He was gnawing the husk of a pod-like fruit as he passed us. Both of them saluted Montgomery.

'Hail,' said they, 'to the Other with the whip!'

'There's a third with a whip now,' said Montgomery. 'So you'd better mind!'

'Was he not made?' said the Ape Man. 'He said – he said he was made.'

The Satyr Man looked curiously at me. 'The Third with the whip, he that walks weeping into the sea, has a thin white face.'

'He has a thin long whip,' said Montgomery.

'Yesterday he bled and wept,' said the Satyr. 'You never bleed nor weep. The Master does not bleed nor weep.'

'Ollendorffian beggar!' said Montgomery. 'You'll bleed and weep if you don't look out.'

'He has five fingers; he is a five-man like me,' said the Ape Man.

'Come along, Prendick,' said Montgomery, taking my arm, and I went on with him.

The Satyr and the Ape Man stood watching us and making other remarks to each other.

'He says nothing,' said the Satyr. 'Men have voices.'

'Yesterday he asked me of things to eat,' said the Ape Man. 'He did not know.' Then they spoke inaudible things, and I heard the Satyr laughing.

It was on our way back that we came upon the dead rabbit. The red body of the wretched little beast was rent to pieces, many of the ribs stripped white, and the backbone indisputably gnawed.

At that Montgomery stopped. 'Good God!' said he, stooping down and picking up some of the crushed vertebræ to examine them more closely. 'Good God!' he repeated, 'what can this mean?'

'Some carnivore of yours has remembered its old habits,' I said, after a pause. 'This backbone has been bitten through.'

He stood staring, with his face white and his lip pulled askew. 'I don't like this,' he said slowly.

'I saw something of the same kind,' said I, 'the first day I came here.'

'The devil you did! What was it?'

'A rabbit with its head twisted off.'

'The day you came here?'

'The day I came here. In the undergrowth, at the back of the enclosure, when I came out in the evening. The head was completely wrung off.'

He gave a long low whistle.

'And what is more, I have an idea which of your brutes did the thing. It's only a suspicion, you know. Before I came on the rabbit I saw one of your monsters drinking in the stream.'

'Sucking his drink?'

'Yes.'

'Not to suck your Drink; *that* is the Law. Much the brutes care for the Law, eh – when Moreau's not about?'

'It was the brute who chased me.'

'Of course,' said Montgomery; 'it's just the way with carnivores. After a kill they drink. It's the taste of blood, you know.

'What was the brute like?' he asked. 'Would you know him again?' He glanced about us, standing astride over the mess of dead rabbit, his eyes roving among the shadows and screens of greenery, the lurking-places and ambuscades of the forest, that abounded us in. 'The taste of blood,' he said again.

He took out his revolver, examined the cartridges in it, and replaced it. Then he began to pull at his dropping lip.

'I think I should know the brute again. I stunned him. He ought to have a handsome bruise on the forehead of him.'

'But then we have to *prove* he killed the rabbit,' said Montgomery. 'I wish I'd never brought the things here.'

I should have gone on, but he stayed there thinking over the mangled rabbit in a puzzled-headed way. As it was, I went to such a distance that the rabbit's remains were hidden.

'Come on!' I said.

Presently he woke up and came towards me. 'You see,' he said, almost in a whisper, 'they are all supposed to have a fixed idea against eating anything that runs on land. If some brute has by accident tasted blood . . .'

We went on some way in silence. 'I wonder what can have happened,' he said to himself. Then, after a pause, again : 'I did a foolish thing the other day. That servant of mine . . . I showed him how to skin and cook a rabbit. It's odd . . . I saw him licking his hands . . . It never occurred to me.'

Then : 'We must put a stop to this. I must tell Moreau.'

He could think of nothing else on our homeward journey.

Moreau took the matter even more seriously than Montgomery, and I need scarcely say I was infected by their evident consternation.

'We must make an example,' said Moreau.

'I've no doubt in my own mind that the Leopard Man was the sinner. But how can we prove it ? I wish, Montgomery, you had kept your taste for meat in hand, and gone without these exciting novelties. We may find ourselves in a mess yet through it.'

'I was a silly ass,' said Montgomery. 'But the thing's done now. And you said I might have them, you know.'

'We must see to the thing at once,' said Moreau. 'I suppose, if anything should turn up, M'ling can take care of himself.'

'I'm not so sure of M'ling,' said Montgomery. 'I think I ought to know him.'

In the afternoon, Moreau, Montgomery, myself, and M'ling went across the island to the huts in the ravine. We three were armed. M'ling carried the little hatchet he used in chopping firewood, and some coils of wire. Moreau had a huge cowherd's horn slung over his shoulder. 'You will see a gathering of the Beast People,' said Montgomery. 'It's a pretty sight.' Moreau said not a word on the way, but his heavy white-fringed face was grimly set.

We crossed the ravine, down which smoked the stream of hot water, and followed the winding pathway through the cane brakes until we reached a wide area covered over with a thick powdery yellow substance, which I believe was sulphur. Above the shoulder of a weedy bank the sea glittered. We came to a kind of shallow natural amphitheatre, and here the four of us halted. Then Moreau sounded the horn and broke the sleeping stillness of the tropical afternoon. He must have had strong lungs. The hooting note rose and rose amidst its echoes to at last an ear-penetrating intensity. 'Ah !' said Moreau, letting the curved instrument fall to his side again.

Immediately there was a crashing through the yellow canes, and a sound of voices from the dense green jungle that marked the morass through which I had run on the previous day. Then at three or four points on the edge of the sulphurous area appeared the grotesque forms of the Beast People, hurrying towards us. I could not help a creeping horror as I perceived first one and then another trot out from the trees or reeds, and come shambling along over the hot dust. But Moreau and Montgomery stood calmly enough, and, perforce, I stuck beside them. First to arrive was the Satyr, strangely unreal, for all that he cast a shadow, and tossed the dust with his hoofs; after him, from the brake, came a monstrous lout, a thing of horse and rhinoceros, chewing a straw as it came; and then appeared the Swine Woman and two Wolf Women; then the Fox-Bear Witch with her red eyes in her peaked red face, and then others – all hurrying eagerly. As they came forward they began to cringe towards Moreau and chant, quite regardless of one another, fragments of the latter half of the litany of the Law : 'His is the Hand that wounds, His is the Hand that heals,' and so forth.

As soon as they had approached within a distance of perhaps thirty yards they halted, and bowing on knees and elbows, began flinging the white dust upon their heads. Imagine the scene if you can. We three blue-clad men, with our misshapen black-faced attendant, standing in a wide expanse of sunlit yellow dust under the blazing blue sky, and surrounded by this circle of crouching and gesticulating monstrosities, some almost human, save in their subtle expression and gestures, some like cripples, some so strangely distorted as to resemble nothing but the denizens of our wildest dreams. And beyond, the reedy lines of a cane brake in one direction, a dense tangle of palm-trees on the other, separating us from the ravine with the huts, and to the north the hazy horizon of the Pacific Ocean.

'Sixty-two, sixty-three,' counted Moreau. 'There are four more.'

'I do not see the Leopard Man,' said I.

Presently Moreau sounded the great horn again, and at the sound of it all the Beast People writhed and grovelled in the dust. Then, slinking out of the cane brake, stooping near the ground, and trying to join the dust-throwing circle behind Moreau's back, came the Leopard Man. And I saw that his forehead was bruised. The last of the Beast People to arrive was the little Ape Man. The earlier animals, hot and weary with their grovelling, shot vicious glances at him.

'Cease,' said Moreau, in his firm loud voice, and the Beast People sat back upon their hams and rested from their worshipping.

'Where is the Sayer of the Law?' said Moreau, and the hairy grey monster bowed his face in the dust.

'Say the words,' said Moreau, and forthwith all in the kneeling assembly, swaying from side to side and dashing up the sulphur with their hands, first the right hand and a puff of dust, and then the left, began once more to chant their strange litany.

When they reached 'Not to eat Flesh or Fish; that is the Law,' Moreau held up his lank white hand. '*Stop!*' he cried, and there fell absolute silence upon them all.

I think they all knew and dreaded what was coming. I looked round at their strange faces. When I saw their wincing attitudes and the furtive dread in their bright eyes, I wondered that I had ever believed them to be men.

'That Law has been broken,' said Moreau.

'None escape,' from the faceless creature with the Silvery Hair. 'None escape,' repeated the kneeling circle of Beast People.

'Who is he?' cried Moreau, and looked round at their faces, cracking his whip. I fancied the Hyæna-Swine looked dejected, so too did the Leopard Man. Moreau stopped, facing this creature, who cringed towards him with the memory and dread of infinite torment. 'Who is he?' repeated Moreau, in a voice of thunder.

'Evil is he who breaks the Law,' chanted the Sayer of the Law.

Moreau looked into the eyes of the Leopard Man, and seemed to be dragging the very soul out of the creature.

'Who breaks the Law – ' said Moreau, taking his eyes off his victim and turning towards us. It seemed to me there was a touch of exultation in his voice.

' – goes back to the House of Pain,' they all clamoured; – 'goes back to the House of Pain, O Master!'

'Back to the House of Pain – back to the House of Pain,' gabbled the Ape Man, as though the idea was sweet to him.

'Do you hear?' said Moreau, turning back to the criminal, 'my friend. . . Hullo!'

For the Leopard Man, released from Moreau's eye, had risen straight from his knees, and now, with eyes aflame and his huge feline tusks flashing out from under his curling lips, leapt towards his tormentor. I am convinced that only the madness of unendurable fear could have prompted this attack. The whole circle of threescore monsters seemed to rise about us. I drew my revolver. The two figures collided. I saw Moreau reeling back from the Leopard Man's blow. There was a furious yelling and howling all about us. Every one was moving rapidly. For a moment I thought it was a general revolt.

The furious face of the Leopard Man flashed by mine, with M'ling close in pursuit. I saw the yellow eyes of the Hyæna-Swine blazing with excitement, his attitude as if he were half-resolved to attack me. The Satyr, too, glared at me over the Hyæna-Swine's hunched shoulders. I heard the crack of Moreau's pistol, and saw the pink flash dart across the tumult. The whole crowd seemed to swing round in the direction of the glint of fire, and I, too, was swung round by the magnetism of the movement. In another second I was running, one of a tumultuous shouting crowd, in pursuit of the escaping Leopard Man.

That is all that I can tell definitely. I saw the Leopard Man strike Moreau, and then everything spun about me, until I was running headlong.

M'ling was ahead, close in pursuit of the fugitive. Behind, their tongues already lolling out, ran the Wolf-Women in great leaping strides. The Swine-Folk followed, squealing with excitement, and the two Bull Men in their swathings of white. Then came Moreau in a cluster of the Beast People, his wide-brimmed straw hat blown off, his revolver in hand, and his lank white hair streaming out. The Hyæna-Swine ran beside me, keeping pace with me, and glancing furtively at me out of his feline eyes, and the others came pattering and shouting behind us.

The Leopard Man went bursting his way through the long canes, which sprang back as he passed and rattled in M'ling's face. We others in the rear found a trampled path for us when we reached the brake. The chase lay through the brake for perhaps a quarter of a mile, and then plunged into a dense thicket, that retarded our movements exceedingly, though we went through it in a crowd together – fronds flicking into our faces, ropy creepers catching us under the chin, or gripping our ankles, thorny plants hooking into and tearing cloth and flesh together.

'He has gone on all-fours through this,' panted Moreau, now just ahead of me.

'None escape,' said the Wolf-Bear, laughing into my face with the exultation of hunting.

We burst out again among rocks, and saw the quarry ahead, running lightly on all-fours, and snarling at us over his shoulder. At that the Wolf-Folk howled with delight. The thing was still clothed, and, at a distance, its face still seemed human, but the carriage of its four limbs was feline, and the furtive droop of its shoulder was distinctly that of a hunted animal. It leapt over some thorny yellow-flowering bushes and was hidden. M'ling was half-way across the space.

Most of us now had lost the first speed of the chase, and had fallen into a longer and steadier stride. I saw, as we traversed the open, that the pursuit was now spreading from a column into a line. The Hyæna-Swine still ran close to me, watching me as it ran, every now and then puckering its muzzle with a snarling laugh.

At the edge of the rocks, the Leopard Man, realising he was making for the projecting cape upon which he had stalked me on the night of my arrival, had doubled in the undergrowth. But Montgomery had seen the manœuvre, and turned him again.

So, panting, tumbling against rocks, torn by brambles, impeded by ferns and reeds, I helped to pursue the Leopard Man, who had broken the Law, and the Hyæna-Swine ran, laughing savagely, by my side. I staggered on, my head reeling, and my heart beating against my ribs, tired almost to death, and yet not daring to lose sight of the chase, lest I should be left alone with this horrible companion. I staggered on in spite of infinite fatigue and the dense heat of the tropical afternoon.

And at last the fury of the hunt slackened. We had pinned the wretched brute into a corner of the island. Moreau, whip in hand, marshalled us all into an irregular line, and we advanced, now slowly, shouting to one another as we advanced, and tightening the cordon about our victim. He lurked, noiseless and invisible, in the bushes through which I had run from him during that midnight pursuit.

'Steady !' cried Moreau ; 'steady !' as the ends of the line crept round the tangle of undergrowth, and hemmed the brute in.

''Ware a rush !' came the voice of Montgomery from beyond the thicket.

I was on the slope above the bushes. Montgomery and Moreau beat along the beach beneath. Slowly we pushed in among the fretted network of branches and leaves. The quarry was silent.

'Back to the House of Pain, the House of Pain, the House of Pain !' yelped the voice of the Ape Man, some twenty yards to the right.

When I heard that I forgave the poor wretch all the fear he had inspired in me.

I heard the twigs snap and the boughs swish aside before the heavy tread of the Horse-Rhinoceros upon my right. Then suddenly, through a polygon of green, in the half-darkness under the luxuriant growth, I saw the creature we were hunting. I halted. He was crouched together into the smallest possible compass, his luminous green eyes turned over his shoulder regarding me.

It may seem a strange contradiction in me – I cannot explain the fact, — but now, seeing the creature there in a perfectly animal attitude, with the light gleaming in its eyes, and its imperfectly human face distorted with terror, I realised again the fact of its humanity. In another moment other of its pursuers would see it, and it would be overpowered and captured, to experience once more the horrible tortures of the enclosure. Abruptly I slipped out my revolver, aimed between its terror-struck eyes, and fired.

As I did so the Hyæna-Swine saw the thing, and flung itself upon it with an eager cry, thrusting thirsty teeth into its neck. All about me the green masses of the thicket were swaying and cracking as the Beast People came rushing together. One face and then another appeared.

'Don't kill it, Prendick,' cried Moreau. 'Don't kill it!' and I saw him stooping as he pushed through under the fronds of the big ferns.

In another moment he had beaten off the Hyæna-Swine with the handle of his whip, and he and Montgomery were keeping away the excited carnivorous Beast People, and particularly M'ling, from the still quivering body. The Hairy Grey Thing came sniffing at the corpse under my arm. The other animals, in their animal ardour, jostled me to get a nearer view.

'Confound you, Prendick!' said Moreau. 'I wanted him.'

'I'm sorry,' said I, though I was not. 'It was the impulse of the moment.' I felt sick with exertion and excitement. Turning, I pushed my way out of the crowding Beast People, and went on alone up the slope towards the higher part of the headland. Under the shouted instructions of Moreau, I heard the three white-swathed Bull Men begin dragging the victim down towards the water.

It was easy now for me to be alone. The Beast People manifested a quite human curiosity about the dead body, and followed it in a thick knot, sniffing and growling at it, as the Bull Men dragged it down the beach. I went to the headland, and watched the Bull Men, black against the evening sky, as they carried the weighted dead body out to sea, and, like a wave across my mind, came the realisation of the unspeakable aimlessness of things upon the island. Upon the beach, among the rocks beneath me, was the Ape Man, the Hyæna-Swine, and several other of the Beast People, standing about Montgomery and Moreau. They were all still intensely excited, and all overflowing with noisy expressions of their loyalty to the Law. Yet I felt an absolute assurance in my own mind that the Hyæna-Swine was implicated in the rabbit-killing. A strange persuasion came upon me that, save for the grossness of the line, the grotesqueness of the forms, I had here before me the whole balance of human life in miniature, the whole interplay of instinct, reason, and fate, in its simplest form. The Leopard Man had happened to go under. That was all the difference.

Poor brutes! I began to see the viler aspect of Moreau's cruelty. I had not thought before of the pain and trouble that came to these poor victims after they had passed from Moreau's hands. I had shivered only at the days of actual torment in the enclosure. But now that seemed to be the lesser part. Before they had been beasts, their instincts fitly adapted to their surroundings, and happy as living things may be. Now they stumbled in the shackles of humanity, lived in a fear that never died, fretted by a law they could not understand; their mock-human existence began in an agony, was one long internal struggle, one long dread of Moreau – and for what? It was the wantonness that stirred me.

Had Moreau had any intelligible object I could have sympathised at least a little with him. I am not so squeamish about pain as that. I could have forgiven him a little even had his motive been hate. But he was so irresponsible, so utterly careless. His curiosity, his mad, aimless investigations, drove him on, and the things were thrown out to live a year or so, to struggle, and blunder, and suffer; at last to die painfully. They were wretched in themselves, the old animal hate moved them to trouble one another, the Law held them back from a brief hot struggle and a decisive end to their natural animosities.

In those days my fear of the Beast People went the way of my personal fear for Moreau. I fell indeed into a morbid state, deep and enduring, alien to fear, which has left permanent scars upon my mind. I must confess I lost faith in the sanity of the world when I saw it suffering the painful disorder of this island. A blind fate, a vast pitiless mechanism, seemed to cut and shape the fabric of existence, and I, Moreau (by his passion for research), Montgomery (by his passion for drink), the Beast People, with their instincts and mental restrictions, were torn and crushed, ruthlessly, inevitably, amid the infinite complexity of its incessant wheels. But this condition did not come all at once . . . I think indeed that I anticipate a little in speaking of it now.

17

A Catastrophe

Scarcely six weeks passed before I had lost every feeling but dislike and abhorrence for these infamous experiments of Moreau's. My one idea was to get away from these horrible caricatures of my Maker's image, back to the sweet and wholesome intercourse of men. My fellow-creatures, from whom I was thus separated, began to assume idyllic virtue and beauty in my memory. My first friendship with Montgomery did not increase. His long separation from humanity, his secret vice of drunkenness, his evident sympathy with the Beast People, tainted him to me. Several times I let him go alone among them. I avoided intercourse with them in every possible way. I spent an increasing proportion of my time upon the beach, looking for some liberating sail that never appeared, until one day there fell upon us an appalling disaster, that put an altogether different aspect upon my strange surroundings.

It was about seven or eight weeks after my landing – rather more, I think, though I had not troubled to keep account of the time – when this catastrophe occurred. It happened in the early morning – I should think about six. I had risen and breakfasted early, having been aroused by the noise of three Beast Men carrying wood into the enclosure.

After breakfast I went to the open gateway of the enclosure and stood there smoking a cigarette and enjoying the freshness of the early morning. Moreau presently came round the corner of the enclosure and greeted me. He passed by me, and I heard him behind me unlock and enter his laboratory. So indurated was I at that time to the abomination of the place, that I heard without a touch of emotion the puma victim begin another day of torture. It met its persecutor with a shriek almost exactly like that of an angry virago.

Then something happened. I do not know what it was exactly to this day. I heard a sharp cry behind me, a fall, and turning, saw an awful face rushing upon me, not human, not animal, but hellish, brown, seamed with red branching scars, red drops starting out upon it, and the lidless eyes ablaze. I flung up my arm to defend myself from the blow that flung me headlong with a broken forearm, and the great monster, swathed in lint and with red-stained bandages fluttering about it, leapt over me and passed. I rolled over and over down the beach, tried to sit up, and collapsed upon my broken arm. Then Moreau appeared, his massive white face all the more terrible for the blood that trickled from his forehead. He carried a revolver in one hand. He scarcely glanced at me, but rushed off at once in pursuit of the puma.

I tried the other arm and sat up. The muffled figure in front ran in great striding leaps along the beach, and Moreau followed her. She turned her head and saw him, then, doubling abruptly, made for the bushes. She gained upon him at every stride. I saw her plunge into them, and Moreau, running slantingly to inter-cept her, fired and missed as she disappeared. Then he too vanished in the green confusion.

I stared after them, and then the pain in my arm flamed up, and with a groan I staggered to my feet. Montgomery appeared in the doorway dressed, and with his revolver in his hand.

'Great God, Prendick!' he said, not noticing that I was hurt. 'That brute's loose! Tore the fetter out of the wall. Have you seen them?' Then sharply, seeing I gripped my arm, 'What's the matter?'

'I was standing in the doorway,' said I.

He came forward and took my arm. 'Blood on the sleeve,' said he, and rolled back the flannel. He pocketed the weapon, felt my arm about painfully, and led me inside. 'Your arm is broken,' he said; and then, 'Tell me exactly how it happened — what happened.'

I told him what I had seen, told him in broken sentences, with gasps of pain between them, and very dexterously and swiftly he bound my arm meanwhile. He slung it from my shoulder, stood back, and looked at me. 'You'll do,' he said. 'And now?'

He thought. Then he went out and locked the gates of the enclosure. He was absent some time.

I was chiefly concerned about my arm. The incident seemed merely one more of many horrible things. I sat down in the deck chair and I must admit, swore heartily at the island. The first dull feeling of injury in my arm had already given way to a burning pain when Montgomery re-appeared.

His face was rather pale, and he showed more of his lower gums than ever. 'I can neither see nor hear anything of him,' he said. 'I've been thinking he may want my help.' He stared at me with his expressionless eyes. 'That was a strong brute,' he said. 'It simply wrenched its fetter out of the wall.'

He went to the window, then to the door, and there turned to me. 'I shall go after him,' he said. 'There's another revolver I can leave with you. To tell you the truth, I feel anxious somehow.'

He obtained the weapon, and put it ready to my hand on the table, then went out, leaving a restless contagion in the air. I did not sit long after he left. I took the revolver in hand and went to the doorway.

The morning was as still as death. Not a whisper of wind was stirring, the sea was like polished glass, the sky empty, the beach desolate. In my half-excited, half-feverish state this stillness of things oppressed me.

I tried to whistle, and the tune died away. I swore again – the second time that morning. Then I went to the corner of the enclosure and stared inland at the green bush that had swallowed up Moreau and Montgomery. When would they return. And how?

Then far away up the beach a little grey Beast Man appeared, ran down to the water's edge, and began splashing about. I strolled back to the doorway, then to the corner again, and so began pacing to and fro like a sentinel upon duty. Once I was arrested by the distant voice of Montgomery bawling, 'Coo-ee . . . Mor-eau !' My arm became less painful, but very hot. I got feverish and thirsty. My shadow grew shorter. I watched the distant figure until it went away again. Would Moreau and

Montgomery never return? Three seabirds began fighting for some stranded treasure.

Then from far away behind the enclosure I heard a pistol-shot. A long silence, and then came another. Then a yelling cry nearer, and another dismal gap of silence. My unfortunate imagination set to work to torment me. Then suddenly a shot close by.

I went to the corner, startled, and saw Montgomery, his face scarlet, his hair disordered, and the knee of his trousers torn. His face expressed profound consternation. Behind him slouched the Beast Man M'ling, and round M'ling's jaws were some ominous brown stains.

'Has he come?' he said.

'Moreau?' said I. 'No.'

'My God!' The man was panting, almost sobbing for breath. 'Go back in,' he said, taking my arm. 'They're mad. They're all rushing about mad. What can have happened? I don't know. I'll tell you when my breath comes. Where's some brandy?'

He limped before me into the room and sat down in the deck chair. M'ling flung himself down just outside the doorway, and began panting like a dog. I got Montgomery some brandy and water. He sat staring blankly in front of him, recovering his breath. After some minutes he began to tell me what had happened.

He had followed their track for some way. It was plain enough at first on account of the crushed and broken bushes, white rags torn from the puma's bandages, and occasional smears of blood on the leaves of the shrubs and undergrowth. He lost the track, however, on the stony ground beyond the stream where I had seen the Beast Man drinking, and went wandering aimlessly westward shouting Moreau's name. Then M'ling had come to him carrying a light hatchet. M'ling had seen nothing of the puma affair. They went on shouting together. Two Beast Men came crouching and peering at them through the undergrowth, with gestures and a furtive carriage that alarmed Montgomery by their strangeness. He hailed them, and they fled guiltily. He stopped shouting after that, and after wandering some time further in an undecided way, determined to visit the huts.

He found the ravine deserted.

Growing more alarmed every minute, he began to retrace his steps. Then it was he encountered the two Swine Men I had seen dancing on the night of my arrival; blood-stained they were about the mouth, and intensely excited. They came crashing through the ferns, and stopped with fierce faces when they saw him. He cracked his whip in some trepidation, and forthwith they rushed at him. Never before had a Beast Man dared to do that. One he shot through the head, M'ling flung himself upon the other, and the two rolled grappling. M'ling got his brute under and with his teeth in its throat, and Montgomery shot that too as it struggled in M'ling's grip. He had some difficulty in inducing M'ling to come on with him.

Thence they had hurried back to me. On the way M'ling had suddenly rushed into a thicket and driven out an under-sized Ocelot Man, also blood-stained, and lame through a wound in the foot. This brute had run a little way and then turned savagely at bay, and Montgomery – with a certain wantonness I thought – had shot him.

'What does it all mean?' said I.

He shook his head and turned once more to the brandy.

18

The Finding of Moreau

When I saw Montgomery swallow a third dose of brandy I took it upon myself to interfere. He was already more than half-fuddled. I told him that some serious thing must have happened to Moreau by this time, or he would have returned, and that it behoved us to ascertain what that catastrophe was. Montgomery raised some feeble objections, and at last agreed. We had some food, and then all three of us started.

It is possibly due to the tension of my mind at the time, but even now that start into the hot stillness of the tropical afternoon is a singularly vivid impression. M'ling went first, his shoulders hunched, his strange black head moving with quick starts as he peered first on this side of the way and then on that. He was unarmed. His axe he had dropped when he encountered the Swine Men. Teeth were *his* weapons when it came to fighting. Montgomery followed with stumbling footsteps, his hands in his pockets, his face downcast; he was in a state of muddled sullenness with me on account of the brandy. My left arm was in a sling – it was lucky it was my left, – and I carried my revolver in my right.

We took a narrow path through the wild luxuriance of the island, going north-westward. And presently M'ling stopped and became rigid with watchfulness. Montgomery almost staggered into him, and then stopped too. Then, listening intently, we heard, coming through the trees, the sound of voices, and footsteps approaching us.

'He is dead,' said a deep vibrating voice.

'He is not dead, he is not dead,' jabbered another.

'We saw, we saw,' said several voices.

'*Hul*-lo!' suddenly shouted Montgomery, 'Hullo there!'

'Confound you!' said I, and gripped my pistol.

There was a silence, then a crashing among the interlacing vegetation, first here, then there, and then half a dozen faces appeared, strange faces, lit by a strange light. M'ling made a growling noise in his throat. I recognised the Ape Man – I had, indeed, already identified his voice – and two of the white-swathed brown-featured creatures I had seen in Montgomery's boat. With them were the two dappled brutes, and that grey horribly crooked creature who said the Law, with grey hair streaming down its cheeks, heavy grey eyebrows, and grey locks pouring off from a central parting upon its sloping forehead, a heavy faceless thing, with strange red eyes, looking at us curiously from amidst the green.

For a space no one spoke. Then Montgomery hiccoughed, 'Who . . . said he was dead?'

The Monkey Man looked guiltily at the Hairy Grey Thing. 'He is dead,' said the monster. 'They saw.'

There was nothing threatening about this detachment at any rate. They seemed awe-stricken and puzzled. 'Where is he?' said Montgomery.

'Beyond,' and the grey creature pointed.

'Is there a Law now?' asked the Monkey Man. 'Is it still to be this and that? Is he dead indeed?' 'Is there a Law?' repeated the man in white. 'Is there a Law, thou Other with the whip? He is dead,' said the Hairy Grey Thing. And they all stood watching us.

'Prendick,' said Montgomery, turning his dull eyes to me. 'He's dead – evidently.'

I had been standing behind him during this colloquy. I began to see how things lay with them. I suddenly stepped in front of him and lifted up my voice: 'Children of the Law,' I said, 'he is *not* dead.'

M'ling turned his sharp eyes on me. 'He has changed his shape – he has changed his body,' I went on. 'For a time you will not see him. He is . . . there' – I pointed upward – 'where he can watch you. You cannot see him. But he can see you. Fear the Law.'

I looked at them squarely. They flinched.

'He is great, he is good,' said the Ape Man, peering fearfully upward among the dense trees.

'And the other Thing?' I demanded.

'The Thing that bled and ran screaming and sobbing – that is dead too,' said the Grey Thing, still regarding me.

'That's well,' grunted Montgomery.

'The Other with the whip,' began the Grey Thing.

'Well?' said I.

'Said he was dead.'

But Montgomery was still sober enough to understand my motive in denying Moreau's death. 'He is not dead,' he said slowly. 'Not dead at all. No more dead than me.'

'Some,' said I, 'have broken the Law. They will die. Some have died. Show us now where his old body lies. The body he cast away because he had no more need of it.'

'It is this way, Man who walked in the Sea,' said the Grey Thing.

And with these six creatures guiding us, we went through the tumult of ferns and creepers and tree-stems towards the north-west. Then came a yelling, a crashing among the branches, and a little pink homunculus rushed by us shrieking. Immediately after appeared a feral monster in headlong pursuit, blood-bedabbled, who was amongst us almost before he could stop his career. The Grey Thing leapt aside; M'ling with a snarl flew at it, and was struck aside; Montgomery fired and missed, bowed his head, threw up his arm, and turned to run. I fired, and the thing still came on; fired again point-blank into its ugly face. I saw its features vanish in a flash. Its face was driven in. Yet it passed me, gripped Montgomery, and holding him, fell headlong beside him, and pulled him sprawling upon itself – in its death-agony.

I found myself alone with M'ling, the dead brute, and the prostrate man. Montgomery raised himself slowly and stared in a muddled way at the shattered Beast Man beside him. It more than half-sobered him. He scrambled to his feet. Then I saw the Grey Thing returning cautiously through the trees.

'See,' said I, pointing to the dead brute. 'Is the Law not alive? This came of breaking the Law.'

He peered at the body. 'He sends the Fire that kills,' said he in his deep voice, repeating part of the ritual.

The others gathered round and stared for a space.

At last we drew near the westward extremity of the island. We came upon the gnawed and mutilated body of the puma, its shoulder-bone smashed by a bullet, and perhaps twenty yards further found at last what we sought. He lay face downward in a trampled space in a cane brake. One hand was almost severed at the wrist, and his silvery hair was dabbled in blood. His head had been battered in by the fetters of the puma. The broken canes beneath him were smeared with blood. His revolver we could not find. Montgomery turned him over.

Resting at intervals, and with the help of the seven Beast People – for he was a heavy man, – we carried him back to the enclosure. The night was darkling. Twice we heard unseen creatures howling and shrieking past our little band, and once the little pink sloth creature appeared and stared at us, and vanished again. But we were not attacked again. At the gates of the enclosure our company of Beast People left us – M'ling going with the rest. We locked ourselves in, and then took Moreau's mangled body into the yard, and laid it upon a pile of brushwood.

Then we went into the laboratory and put an end to all we found living there.

19

Montgomery's 'Bank Holiday'

When this was accomplished, and we had washed and eaten, Montgomery and I went into my little room and seriously discussed our position for the first time. It was then near midnight. He was almost sober, but greatly disturbed in his mind. He had been strangely under the influence of Moreau's personality. I do not think it had ever occurred to him that Moreau could die. This disaster was the sudden collapse of the habits that had become part of his nature in the ten or more monotonous years he had spent on the island. He talked vaguely, answered my questions crookedly, wandered into general questions.

'This silly ass of a world,' he said. 'What a muddle it all is! I haven't had any life. I wonder when it's going to begin. Sixteen years being bullied by nurses and schoolmasters at their own sweet will, five in London grinding hard at medicine – bad food, shabby lodgings, shabby clothes, shabby vice – a blunder – *I* didn't know any better – and hustled off to this beastly island. Ten years here! What's it all for, Prendick? Are we bubbles blown by a baby?'

It was hard to deal with such ravings. 'The thing we have to think of now,' said I, 'is how to get away from this island.'

'What's the good of getting away? I'm an outcast. Where am *I* to join on? It's all very well for *you*, Prendick. Poor old Moreau! We can't leave him here to have his bones picked. As it is ... And besides, what will become of the decent part of the Beast Folk?'

'Well,' said I. 'That will do to-morrow. I've been thinking we might make the brushwood into a pyre and burn his body – and those other things ... Then what will happen with the Beast Folk?'

'*I* don't know. I suppose those that were made of beasts of prey will make silly asses of themselves sooner or later. We can't massacre the lot. Can we? I suppose that's what *your* humanity would suggest? . . . But they'll change. They are sure to change.'

He talked thus inconclusively until at last I felt my temper going. 'Damnation!' he exclaimed, at some petulance of mine. 'Can't you see I'm in a worse hole than you are?' And he got up and went for the brandy. 'Drink,' he said, returning. 'You logic-chopping, chalky-faced saint of an atheist, drink.'

'Not I,' said I, and sat grimly watching his face under the yellow paraffin flame as he drank himself into a garrulous misery. I have a memory of infinite tedium. He wandered into a maudlin defence of the Beast People and of M'ling. M'ling, he said, was the only thing that had ever really cared for him. And suddenly an idea came to him.

'I'm damned!' said he, staggering to his feet, and clutching the brandy-bottle. By some flash of intuition I knew what it was he intended. 'You don't give drink to that beast!' I said, rising and facing him.

'Beast!' said he. 'You're the beast. He takes his liquor like a Christian. Come out of the way, Prendick.'

'For God's sake,' said I.

'*Get* . . . out of the way,' he roared, and suddenly whipped out his revolver.

'Very well,' said I, and stood aside, half-minded to fall upon him as he put his hand upon the latch, but deterred by the thought of my useless arm. 'You've made a beast of yourself. To the beasts you may go.'

He flung the doorway open and stood, half-facing me, between the yellow lamp-light and the pallid glare of the moon; his eye-sockets were blotches of black under his stubbly eye-brows. 'You're a solemn prig, Prendick, a silly ass! You're always fearing and fancying. We're on the edge of things. I'm bound to cut my throat to-morrow. I'm going to have a damned good bank holiday to-night.'

He turned and went out into the moonlight. 'M'ling,' he cried; 'M'ling, old friend!'

Three dim creatures in the silvery light came along the edge of the wan beach, one a white-wrapped creature, the other two blotches of blackness following it. They halted, staring. Then I saw M'ling's hunched shoulders as he came round the corner of the house.

'Drink,' cried Montgomery; 'drink, ye brutes! Drink, and be men. Dammy, I'm the cleverest! Moreau forgot this. This is the last touch. Drink, I tell you.' And waving the bottle in his hand, he started off at a kind of quick trot to the westward, M'ling ranging himself between him and the three dim creatures who followed.

I went to the doorway. They were already indistinct in the mist of the moonlight before Montgomery halted. I saw him administer a dose of the raw brandy to M'ling, and saw the five figures melt into one vague patch. 'Sing,' I heard Montgomery shout; 'sing all together, "Confound old Prendick." . . . That's right. Now, again: "Confound old Prendick."'

The black group broke up into five separate figures and wound slowly away from me along the band of shining beach. Each went howling at his own sweet will, yelping insult at me, or giving whatever other vent this new inspiration of brandy demanded.

Presently I heard Montgomery's remote voice shouting, 'Right turn!' and they passed with their shouts and howls into the blackness of the landward trees. Slowly, very slowly, they receded into silence.

The peaceful splendour of the night healed again. The moon was now past the meridian and travelling down the west. It was at its full, and very bright, riding through the empty blue sky. The shadow of the wall lay, a yard wide, and of inky blackness, at my feet. The eastward sea was a featureless grey, dark and mysterious, and between the sea and the shadow the grey sands (of volcanic glass and crystals), flashed and shone like a beach of diamonds. Behind me the paraffin lamp flared hot and ruddy.

Then I shut the door, locked it, and went into the enclosure where Moreau lay beside his latest victims – the staghounds and the llama, and some other wretched brutes, – his massive face, calm even after his terrible death, and with the hard eyes open, staring at the dead white moon above. I sat down upon the edge of the sink, and, with my eyes upon that ghastly pile of silvery light and ominous shadows, began to turn over my plans in my mind.

In the morning I would gather some provisions in the dingey, and after setting fire to the pyre before me, push out into the desolation of the high sea once more. I felt that for Montgomery there was no help; that he was in truth half akin to these Beast Folk, unfitted for human kindred. I do not know how long I sat there scheming. It must have been an hour or so. Then my planning was interrupted by the return of Montgomery to my neighbourhood. I heard a yelling from many throats, a tumult of exultant cries, passing down towards the beach, whooping and howling and excited shrieks, that seemed to come to a stop near the water's edge. The riot rose and fell; I heard heavy blows and the splintering smash of wood, but it did not trouble me then. A discordant chanting began.

My thoughts went back to my means of escape. I got up, brought the lamp, and went into a shed to look at some kegs I had seen there. Then I became interested in the contents of some biscuit tins, and opened one. I saw something out of the tail of my eye, a red figure, and turned sharply.

Behind me lay the yard, vividly black and white in the moonlight, and the pile of wood and fagots on which Moreau and his mutilated victims lay, one on another. They seemed to be gripping one another in one last revengeful grapple. His wounds gaped black as night, and the blood that had dripped lay in black patches upon the sand. Then I saw, without understanding, the cause of the phantom, a ruddy glow that came and danced and went upon the wall opposite. I misinterpreted this, fancied it was a reflection of my flickering lamp, and turned again to the stores in the shed. I went on rummaging among them as well as a one-armed man could, finding this convenient thing and that, and putting them aside for to-morrow's launch. My movements were slow, and the time passed quickly. Presently the daylight crept upon me.

The chanting died down, gave place to a clamour, then began again, and suddenly broke into a tumult. I heard cries of 'More, more!' a sound like quarrelling, and a sudden wild shriek. The quality of the sounds changed so greatly that it arrested my attention. I went out into the yard and listened. Then, cutting like a knife across the confusion, came the crack of a revolver.

I rushed at once through my room to the little doorway. As I did so I heard some of the packing-cases behind me go sliding down and smash together, with a clatter of glass on the floor of the shed. But I did not heed these. I flung the door open and looked out.

Up the beach by the boathouse a bonfire was burning, raining up sparks into the indistinctness of the dawn. Around this struggled a mass of black figures. I heard Montgomery call my name. I began to run at once towards this fire, revolver in hand. I saw the pink tongue of Montgomery's pistol lick out once, close to the ground. He was down. I shouted with all my strength and fired into the air.

I heard some one cry 'The Master!' The knotted black struggle broke into scattering units, the fire leapt and sank down. The crowd of Beast People fled in sudden panic before me up the beach. In my excitement I fired at their retreating backs as they disappeared among the bushes. Then I turned to the black heaps upon the ground.

Montgomery lay on his back with the hairy grey Beast Man sprawling across his body. The brute was dead, but still gripping Montgomery's throat with its curving claws. Near by lay M'ling on his face, and quite still, his neck bitten open, and the upper part of the smashed brandy-bottle in his hand. Two other figures lay near the fire, the one motionless, the other groaning fitfully, every now and then raising its head slowly, then dropping it again.

I caught hold of the Grey Man and pulled him off Montgomery's body; his claws drew down the torn coat reluctantly as I dragged him away.

Montgomery was dark in the face and scarcely breathing. I splashed sea-water on his face, and pillowed his head on my rolled-up coat. M'ling was dead. The wounded creature by the fire – it was a Wolf Brute with a bearded grey face – lay, I found, with the fore part of its body upon the still glowing timber. The wretched thing was injured so dreadfully that in mercy I blew its brains out at once. The other brute was one of the Bull Men swathed in white. He too was dead.

The rest of the Beast People had vanished from the beach. I went to Montgomery again and knelt beside him, cursing my ignorance of medicine.

The fire beside me had sunk down, and only charred beams of timber glowing at the central ends, and mixed with a grey ash of brushwood, remained. I wondered casually where Montgomery had got his wood. Then I saw that the dawn was upon us. The sky had grown brighter, the setting moon was growing pale and opaque in the luminous blue of the day. The sky to the eastward was rimmed with red.

Then I heard a thud and a hissing behind me, and looking round, sprang to my feet with a cry of horror. Against the warm dawn great tumultuous masses of black smoke were boiling up out of the enclosure, and through their stormy darkness shot flickering threads of blood-red flame. Then the thatched roof caught. I saw the curving charge of the flames across the sloping straw. A spurt of fire jetted from the window of my room.

I knew at once what had happened. I remembered the crash I had heard. When I had rushed out to Montgomery's assistance I had overturned the lamp.

The hopelessness of saving any of the contents of the enclosure stared me in the face. My mind came back to my plan of flight, and turning swiftly I looked to see where the two boats lay upon the beach. They were gone ! Two axes lay upon the sands beside me, chips and splinters were scattered broadcast, and the ashes of the bonfire were blackening and smoking under the dawn. He had burnt the boats to revenge himself upon me and prevent our return to mankind.

A sudden convulsion of rage shook me. I was almost moved to batter his foolish head in as he lay there helpless at my feet. Then suddenly his hand moved, so feebly, so pitifully, that my wrath vanished. He groaned and opened his eyes for a minute.

I knelt down beside him and raised his head. He opened his eyes again, staring silently at the dawn, and then they met mine. The lids fell, 'Sorry,' he said presently, with an effort. He seemed trying to think. 'The last,' he murmured, 'the last of this silly universe. What a mess – '

I listened. His head fell helplessly to one side. I thought some drink might revive him, but there was neither drink nor vessel in which to bring drink at hand. He seemed suddenly heavier. My heart went cold.

I bent down to his face, put my hand through the rent in his blouse. He was dead; and even as he died a line of white heat, the limb of the sun, rose eastward beyond the projection of the bay, splashing its radiance across the sky, and turning the dark sea into a weltering tumult of dazzling light. It fell like a glory upon his death-shrunken face.

I let his head fall gently upon the rough pillow I had made for him, and stood up. Before me was the glittering desolation of the sea, the awful solitude upon which I had already suffered so much; behind me the island, hushed under the dawn, its Beast People silent and unseen. The enclosure with all its provisions and ammunition burnt noisily, with sudden gusts of flame, a fitful crackling, and now and then a crash. The heavy smoke drove up the beach away from me, rolling low over the distant tree-tops towards the huts in the ravine. Beside me were the charred vestiges of the boats and these five dead bodies.

Then out of the bushes came three Beast People, with hunched shoulders, protruding heads, misshapen hands awkwardly held, and inquisitive unfriendly eyes, and advanced towards me with hesitating gestures.

20

Alone with the Beast Folk

I faced these people, facing my fate in them, single-handed – now literally single-handed, for I had a broken arm. In my pocket was a revolver with two empty chambers. Among the chips scattered about the beach lay the two axes that had been used to chop up the boats. The tide was creeping in behind me.

There was nothing for it but courage. I looked squarely into the faces of the advancing monsters. They avoided my eyes, and their quivering nostrils investigated the bodies that lay beyond me on the beach. I took half a dozen steps, picked up the blood-stained whip that lay beneath the body of the Wolf Man, and cracked it.

They stopped and stared at me. 'Salute,' said I. 'Bow down!'

They hesitated. One bent his knees. I repeated my command, with my heart in my mouth, and advanced upon them. One knelt, then the other two.

I turned and walked towards the dead bodies, keeping my face towards the three kneeling Beast Men, very much as an actor passing up the stage faces his audience.

'They broke the Law,' said I, putting my foot on the Sayer of the Law. 'They have been slain. Even the Sayer of the Law. Even the Other with the whip. Great is the Law! Come and see.'

'None escape,' said one of them, advancing and peering.

'None escape,' said I. 'Therefore hear and do as I command.' They stood up, looking questioningly at one another.

'Stand there,' said I.

I picked up the hatchets and swung them by their heads from the sling of my arm, turned Montgomery over, picked up his revolver, still loaded in two chambers, and bending down to rummage, found half a dozen cartridges in his pocket.

'Take him,' said I, standing up again and pointing with the whip; 'take him and carry him out, and cast him into the sea.'

They came forward, evidently still afraid of Montgomery, but still more afraid of my cracking red whip-lash, and, after some fumbling and hesitation, some whip-cracking and shouting, lifted him gingerly, carried him down to the beach, and went splashing into the dazzling welter of the sea. 'On,' said I, 'on! – carry him far.'

They went in up to their armpits and stood regarding me. 'Let go,' said I, and the body of Montgomery vanished with a splash. Something seemed to tighten across my chest. 'Good!' said I, with a break in my voice, and they came back, hurrying and fearful, to the margin of the water, leaving long wakes of black in the silver. At the water's edge they stopped, turning and glaring into the sea as though they presently expected Montgomery to arise thencefrom and exact vengeance.

'Now these,' said I, pointing to the other bodies.

They took care not to approach the place where they had thrown Montgomery into the water, but, instead, carried the four dead Beast People slantingly along the beach for perhaps a hundred yards before they waded out and cast them away.

As I watched them disposing of the mangled remains of M'ling I heard a light footfall behind me, and turning quickly saw the big Hyæna-Swine perhaps a dozen yards away. His head was bent down, his bright eyes were fixed upon me, his stumpy hands clenched and held close by his side. He stopped in this crouching attitude when I turned, his eyes a little averted.

For a moment we stood eye to eye. I dropped the whip and snatched at the pistol in my pocket. For I meant to kill this brute – the most formidable of any left now upon the island – at the first excuse. It may seem treacherous, but so I was resolved. I was far more afraid of him than of any other two of the Beast Folk. His continued life was, I knew, a threat against mine.

I was perhaps a dozen seconds collecting myself. Then I cried, 'Salute! Bow down!'

His teeth flashed upon me in a snarl. 'Who are *you*, that I should . . .'

Perhaps a little too spasmodically, I drew my revolver, aimed, and quickly fired. I heard him yelp, saw him run sideways and turn, knew I had missed, and clicked back the cock with my thumb for the next shot. But he was already running headlong, jumping from side to side, and I dared not risk another miss. Every now and then he looked back at me over his shoulder. He went slanting along the beach, and vanished beneath the driving masses of dense smoke that were still pouring out from the burning enclosure. For some time I stood staring after him. I turned to my three obedient Beast Folk again, and signalled them to drop the body they still carried. Then I went back to the place by the fire where the bodies had fallen, and kicked the sand until all the brown blood-stains were absorbed and hidden.

I dismissed my three serfs with a wave of the hand, and went up the beach into the thickets. I carried my pistol in my hand, my whip thrust, with the hatchets, in the sling of my arm. I was anxious to be alone, to think out the position in which I was now placed.

A dreadful thing, that I was only beginning to realise, was that over all this island there was now no safe place where I could be alone, and secure to rest or sleep. I had recovered strength amazingly since my landing, but I was still inclined to be nervous, and to break down under any great stress. I felt I ought to cross the island, and establish myself with the Beast People, making myself secure in their confidence. And my heart failed me. I went back to the beach, and, turning eastward past the burning enclosure, made for a point where a shallow spit of coral sand ran out towards the reef. Here I could sit down and think, my back to the sea, and my face against any surprise. And there I sat, chin on knees, the sun beating down upon my head, and a growing dread in my mind, plotting how I could live on against the hour of my rescue (if ever rescue came). I tried to review the whole situation as calmly as I could, but it was impossible to clear the thing of emotion.

I began turning over in my mind the reason of Montgomery's despair. 'They will change,' he said. 'They are sure to change.' And Moreau – what was it that Moreau had said? The stubborn beast flesh grows day by day back again . . .' Then I came round to the Hyæna-Swine. I felt assured that if I did not kill that brute

he would kill me. The Sayer of the Law was dead – worse luck!
. . . They knew now that we of the Whips could be killed, even
as they themselves were killed . . .

Were they peering at me already out of the green masses of
ferns and palms over yonder – watching until I came within
their spring? Were they plotting against me? What was the
Hyæna-Swine telling them? My imagination was running away
with me into a morass of unsubstantial fears.

My thoughts were disturbed by a crying of sea-birds, hurrying
towards some black object that had been stranded by the waves
on the beach near the enclosure. I knew what that object was,
but I had not the heart to go back and drive them off. I began
walking along the beach in the opposite direction, designing to
come round the eastward corner of the island, and so approach
the ravine of the huts, without traversing the possible ambuscades of the thickets.

Perhaps half a mile along the beach I became aware of one of
my three Beast Folk advancing out of the landward bushes
towards me. I was now so nervous with my own imaginings
that I immediately drew my revolver. Even the propitiatory
gestures of the creature failed to disarm me.

He hesitated as he approached. 'Go away.' cried I. There was
something very suggestive of a dog in the cringing attitude of
the creature. It retreated a little way, very like a dog being sent
home, and stopped, looking at me imploringly with canine
brown eyes. 'Go away,' said I. 'Do not come near me.'

'May I not come near you?' it said.

'No. Go away.' I insisted, and snapped my whip. Then,
putting my whip in my teeth, I stooped for a stone, and with
that threat drove the creature away.

So, in solitude, I came round by the ravine of the Beast People,
and, hiding among the weeds and reeds that separated this
crevice from the sea, I watched such of them as appeared, trying
to judge from their gestures and appearance how the death of
Moreau and Montgomery and the destruction of the House of
Pain had affected them. I know now the folly of my cowardice.
Had I kept my courage up to the level of the dawn, had I not
allowed it to ebb away in solitary thought, I might have grasped

the vacant sceptre of Moreau, and ruled over the Beast People. As it was, I lost the opportunity, and sank to the position of a mere leader among my fellows.

Towards noon certain of them came and squatted basking in the hot sand. The imperious voices of hunger and thirst prevailed over my dread. I came out of the bushes, and, revolver in hand, walked down towards these seated figures. One, a Wolf Woman, turned her head and stared at me, and then the others. None attempted to rise or salute me. I felt too faint and weary to insist against so many, and I let the moment pass.

'I want food,' said I, almost apologetically, and drawing near.

'There is food in the huts,' said an Ox-Boar Man drowsily, and looking away from me.

I passed them, and went down into the shadow and odours of the almost deserted ravine. In an empty hut I feasted on some fruit, and then, after I had propped some specked and half-decayed branches and sticks about the opening, and placed myself with my face towards it, and my hand upon my revolver, the exhaustion of the last thirty hours claimed its own, and I let myself fall into a light slumber, trusting that the flimsy barricade I had erected would cause sufficient noise in its removal to save me from surprise.

21

The Reversion of the Beast Folk

In this way I became one among the Beast People in the Island of Doctor Moreau. When I awoke it was dark about me. My arm ached in its bandages. I sat up, wondering at first where I might be. I heard coarse voices talking outside. Then I saw that my barricade had gone, and that the opening of the hut stood clear. My revolver was still in my hand.

I heard something breathing, saw something crouched together close beside me. I held my breath, trying to see what it was. It began to move slowly, interminably. Then something soft and warm and moist passed across my hand.

All my muscles contracted. I snatched my hand away. A cry of alarm began, and was stifled in my throat. Then I just realised what had happened sufficiently to stay my fingers on the revolver.

'Who is that?' I said in a hoarse whisper, the revolver still pointed.

'I, Master.'

'Who are you?'

'They say there is no Master now. But I know, I know. I carried the bodies into the sea, O Walker in the Sea, the bodies of those you slew. I am your slave, Master.'

'Are you the one I met on the beach?' I asked.

'The same, Master.'

The thing was evidently faithful enough, for it might have fallen upon me as I slept. 'It is well,' I said, extending my hand for another licking kiss. I began to realise what its presence meant, and the tide of my courage flowed. 'Where are the others?' I asked.

'They are mad. They are fools,' said the Dog Man. 'Even now they talk together beyond there. They say "The Master is dead;

the Other with the Whip is dead. That Other who walked in the Sea is – as we are. We have no Master, no Whips, no House of Pain any more. There is an end. We love the Law, and will keep it; but there is no pain, no Master, no Whips for ever again." So they say. But I know, Master, I know.'

I felt in the darkness and patted the Dog Man's head. 'It is well,' I said again.

'Presently you will slay them all,' said the Dog Man.

'Presently,' I answered. 'I will slay them all – after certain days and certain things have come to pass. Every one of them save those you spare, every one of them shall be slain.'

'What the Master wishes to kill the Master kills,' said the Dog Man with a certain satisfaction in his voice.

'And that their sins may grow,' I said; 'let them live in their folly until their time is ripe. Let them not know that I am the Master.'

'The Master's will is sweet,' said the Dog Man, with the ready tact of his canine blood.

'But one has sinned,' said I. 'Him I will kill, whenever I may meet him. When I say to you, "That is he," see that you fall upon him. – And now I will go to the men and women who are assembled together.'

For a moment the opening of the hut was blackened by the exit of the Dog Man. Then I followed and stood up, almost in the exact spot where I had been when I had heard Moreau and his staghound pursuing me. But now it was night, and all the miasmatic ravine about me was black, and beyond, instead of a green sunlit slope, I saw a red fire before which hunched grotesque figures moved to and fro. Further were the thick trees, a bank of black fringed above with the black lace of the upper branches. The moon was just riding up on the edge of the ravine, and like a bar across its face drove the spire of vapour that was for ever streaming from the fumarolles of the island.

'Walk by me,' said I, nerving myself, and side by side we walked down the narrow way, taking little heed of the dim things that peered at us out of the huts.

None about the fire attempted to salute me. Most of them disregarded me – ostentatiously. I looked round for the Hyæna-

Swine, but he was not there. Altogether, perhaps, twenty of the Beast Folk squatted, staring into the fire or talking to one another.

'He is dead, he is dead, the Master is dead,' said the voice of the Ape Man to the right of me. 'The House of Pain – there *is* no House of Pain.'

'He is not dead,' said I, in a loud voice. 'Even now he watches us.'

This startled them. Twenty pairs of eyes regarded me.

'The House of Pain is gone,' said I. 'It will come again. The Master you cannot see. Yet even now he listens above you.'

'True, true!' said the Dog Man.

They were staggered at my assurance. An animal may be ferocious and cunning enough, but it takes a real man to tell a lie. 'The Man with the Bandaged Arm speaks a strange thing,' said one of the Beast Folk.

'I tell you it is so,' I said. 'The Master and the House of Pain will come again. Woe be to him who breaks the Law!'

They looked curiously at one another. With an affectation of indifference I began to chop idly at the ground in front of me with my hatchet. They looked, I noticed, at the deep cuts I made in the turf.

Then the Satyr raised a doubt; I answered him, and then one of the dappled things objected, and an animated discussion sprang up round the fire. Every moment I began to feel more convinced of my present security. I talked now without the catching in my breath, due to the intensity of my excitement, that had troubled me at first. In the course of about an hour I had really convinced several of the Beast Folk of the truth of my assertions, and talked most of the others into a dubious state. I kept a sharp eye for my enemy the Hyæna-Swine, but he never appeared. Every now and then a suspicious movement would startle me, but my confidence grew rapidly. Then as the moon crept down from the zenith, one by one the listeners began to yawn (showing the oddest teeth in the light of the sinking fire), and first one, and then another, retired towards the den in the ravine. And I, dreading the silence and darkness, went with them, knowing I was safer with several of them than with one alone.

In this manner began the longer part of my sojourn upon this Island of Doctor Moreau. But from that night until the end came there was but one thing happened to tell, save a series of innumerable small unpleasant details and the fretting of an incessant uneasiness. So that I prefer to make no chronicle for that gap of time, to tell only one cardinal incident of the ten months I spent as an intimate of these half-humanised brutes. There is much that sticks in my memory that I could write, things that I would cheerfully give my right hand to forget. But they do not help the telling of the story. In the retrospect it is strange to remember how soon I fell in with these monsters' ways and gained my confidence again. I had my quarrels, of course, and could show some teeth-marks still, but they soon gained a wholesome respect for my trick of throwing stones and the bite of my hatchet. And my St Bernard Dog Man's loyalty was of infinite service to me. I found their simple scale of honour was based mainly on the capacity for inflicting trenchant wounds. Indeed I may say – without vanity, I hope – that I held something like a pre-eminence among them. One or two whom, in various disputes, I had scarred rather badly, bore me a grudge, but it vented itself chiefly behind my back, and at a safe distance from my missiles, in grimaces.

The Hyæna-Swine avoided me, and I was always on the alert for him. My inseparable Dog Man hated and dreaded him intensely. I really believe that was at the root of the brute's attachment to me. It was soon evident to me that the former monster had tasted blood, and gone the way of the Leopard Man. He formed a lair somewhere in the forest, and became solitary. Once I tried to induce the Beast Folk to hunt him, but I lacked the authority to make them co-operate for one end. Again and again I tried to approach his den and come upon him unawares, but always he was too acute for me, and saw or winded me and got away. He too made every forest pathway dangerous to me and my allies with his lurking ambuscades. The Dog Man scarcely dared to leave my side.

In the first month or so the Beast Folk, compared with their latter condition, were human enough, and for one or two besides my canine friend I even conceived a friendly tolerance. The little pink sloth creature displayed an odd affection for me, and took to following me about. The Monkey Man bored me, however. He assumed, on the strength of his five digits, that he was my equal, and was for ever jabbering at me, jabbering the most arrant nonsense. One thing about him entertained me a little: he had a fantastic trick of coining new words. He had an idea, I believe, that to gabble about names that meant nothing was the proper use of speech. He called it 'big thinks,' to distinguish it from 'little thinks' – the sane everyday interests of life. If ever I made a remark he did not understand, he would praise it very much, ask me to say it again, learn it by heart, and go off repeating it, with a word wrong here or there, to all the milder of the Beast People. He thought nothing of what was plain and comprehensible. I invented some very curious 'big thinks' for his especial use. I think now that he was the silliest creature I ever met; he had developed in the most wonderful way the distinctive silliness of man without losing one jot of the natural folly of a monkey.

This, I say, was in the earlier weeks of my solitude among these brutes. During that time they respected the usage established by the Law, and behaved with general decorum. Once I found another rabbit torn to pieces – by the Hyæna-Swine, I am assured, – but that was all. It was about May when I first distinctly perceived a growing difference in their speech and carriage, a growing coarseness of articulation, a growing disinclination to talk. My Monkey Man's jabber multiplied in volume, but grew less and less comprehensible, more and more simian. Some of the others seemed altogether slipping their hold upon speech, though they still understood what I said to them at that time. Can you imagine language, once clearcut and exact, softening and guttering, losing shape and import, becoming mere lumps of sound again? And they walked erect with an increasing difficulty. Though they evidently felt ashamed of themselves, every now and then I would come upon one or other running on toes and finger-tips, and quite unable to recover the vertical attitude. They held things more clumsily; drinking by suction, feeding by gnawing; grew commoner every day. I realised more keenly than ever what Moreau had told me about the 'stubborn beast flesh.' They were reverting, and reverting very rapidly.

Some of them – the pioneers, I noticed with some surprise, were all females – began to disregard the injunction of decency – deliberately for the most part. Others even attempted public outrages upon the institution of monogamy. The tradition of the Law was clearly losing its force. I cannot pursue this disagreeable subject. My Dog Man imperceptibly slipped back to the dog again; day by day he became dumb, quadrupedal, hairy. I scarcely noticed the transition from the companion on my right hand to the lurching dog at my side. As the carelessness and disorganisation increased from day to day, the lane of dwelling-places, at no time very sweet, became so loathsome that I left it, and going across the island made myself a hovel of boughs amid the black ruins of Moreau's enclosure. Some memory of pain, I found, still made that place the safest from the Beast Folk.

It would be impossible to detail every step of the lapsing of these monsters; to tell how, day by day, the human semblance left them; how they gave up bandagings and wrappings, abandoned at last every stitch of clothing; how the hair began to spread over the exposed limbs; how their foreheads fell away and their faces projected; how the quasi-human intimacy I had permitted myself with some of them in the first month of my loneliness became a horror to recall.

The change was slow and inevitable. For them and for me it came without any definite shock. I still went among them in safety, because no jolt in the downward glide had released the increasing charge of explosive animalism that ousted the human day by day. But I began to fear that soon now that shock must come. My St Bernard Brute followed me to the enclosure, and his vigilance enabled me to sleep at times in something like peace. The little pink sloth thing became shy and left me, to crawl back to its natural life once more among the tree-branches. We were in just the state of equilibrium that would remain in one of those 'Happy Family' cages that animal-tamers exhibit, if the tamer were to leave it for ever.

Of course these creatures did not decline into such beasts as the reader has seen in zoological gardens – into ordinary bears, wolves, tigers, oxen, swine, and apes. There was still something strange about each; in each Moreau had blended this animal with that; one perhaps was ursine chiefly, another feline chiefly, another bovine chiefly, but each was tainted with other creatures – a kind of generalised animalism appeared through the specific dispositions. And the dwindling shreds of the humanity still startled me every now and then, a momentary recrudescence of speech perhaps, an unexpected dexterity of the forefeet, a pitiful attempt to walk erect.

I too must have undergone strange changes. My clothes hung about me as yellow rags, through whose rents glowed the tanned skin. My hair grew long, and became matted together. I am told that even now my eyes have a strange brightness, a swift alertness of movement.

At first I spent the daylight hours on the southward beach watching for a ship, hoping and praying for a ship. I counted on the *Ipecacuanha* returning as the year wore on, but she never came. Five times I saw sails, and thrice smoke, but nothing ever touched the island. I always had a bonfire ready, but no doubt the volcanic reputation of the island was taken to account for that.

It was only about September or October that I began to think of making a raft. By that time my arm had healed, and both my hands were at my service again. At first I found my helplessness appalling. I had never done any carpentry or suchlike work in my life, and I spent day after day in experimental chopping and binding among the trees. I had no ropes, and could hit on nothing wherewith to make ropes; none of the abundant creepers seemed limber or strong enough, and with all my litter of scientific education I could not devise any way of making them so. I spent more than a fortnight grubbing among the black ruins of the enclosure and on the beach where the boats had been burnt, looking for nails and other stray pieces of metal that might prove of service. Now and then some Beast creature would watch me, and go leaping off when I called to it. There came a season of thunderstorms and heavy rain that greatly retarded my work, but at last the raft was completed.

I was delighted with it. But with a certain lack of practical sense that has always been my bane I had made it a mile or more from the sea, and before I had dragged it down to the beach the thing had fallen to pieces. Perhaps it is as well that I was saved from launching it. But at the time my misery at my failure was so acute, that for some days I simply moped on the beach and stared at the water and thought of death.

But I did not mean to die, and an incident occurred that warned me unmistakably of the folly of letting the days pass so – for each fresh day was fraught with increasing danger from the Beast Monsters. I was lying in the shade of the enclosure wall staring out to sea, when I was startled by something cold touching the skin of my heel, and starting round found the little pink sloth creature blinking into my face. He had long since lost speech and active movement, and the lank hair of the little brute grew thicker every day, and his stumpy claws more askew. He made a moaning noise when he saw he had attracted my attention, went a little way towards the bushes, and looked back at me.

At first I did not understand, but presently it occurred to me that he wished me to follow him, and this I did at last, slowly – for the day was hot. When he reached the trees he clambered into them, for he could travel better among their swinging creepers than on the ground.

And suddenly in a trampled space I came upon a ghastly group. My St Bernard creature lay on the ground dead, and near his body crouched the Hyæna-Swine, gripping the quivering flesh with misshapen claws, gnawing at it and snarling with delight. As I approached the monster lifted its glaring eyes to mine, its lips went trembling back from its red-stained teeth, and it growled menacingly. It was not afraid and not ashamed; the last vestige of the human taint had vanished. I advanced a step further, stopped, pulled out my revolver. At last I had him face to face.

The brute made no sign of retreat. But its ears went back, its hair bristled, and its body crouched together. I aimed between the eyes and fired. As I did so the thing rose straight at me in a leap, and I was knocked over like a ninepin. It clutched at me with its crippled hand, and struck me in the face. Its spring carried it over me. I fell under the hind part of its body, but luckily I had hit as I meant, and it had died even as it leapt. I crawled out from under its unclean weight and stood up trembling, staring at its quivering body. That danger at least was over. But this, I knew, was only the first of the series of relapses that must come.

I burnt both the bodies on a pyre of brushwood. Now, indeed, I saw clearly that unless I left the island my death was only a question of time. The Beasts by that time had, with one or two exceptions, left the ravine, and made themselves lairs, according to their tastes, among the thickets of the island. Few prowled by day; most of them slept, and the island might have seemed deserted to a newcomer; but at night the air was hideous with their calls and howling. I had half a mind to make a massacre of them – to build traps or fight them with my knife. Had I possessed sufficient cartridges, I should not have hesitated to begin the killing. There could now be scarcely a score left of the dangerous carnivores; the braver of these were already dead. After the death of this poor dog of mine, my last friend, I too adopted to some extent the practice of slumbering in the daytime, in order to be on my guard at night. I rebuilt my den in the walls of the enclosure with such a narrow opening that anything attempting to enter must necessarily make a considerable noise. The creatures had lost the art of fire, too, and recovered their fear of it. I turned once more, almost passionately now, to hammering together stakes and branches to form a raft for my escape.

I found a thousand difficulties. I am an extremely unhandy man – my schooling was over before the days of Slöjd, – but most of the requirements of a raft I met at last in some clumsy circuitous way or other, and this time I took care of the strength. The only insurmountable obstacle was, that I had no vessel to contain the water I should need if I floated forth upon these untravelled seas. I would have even tried pottery, but the island contained no clay. I used to go moping about the island, trying with all my might to solve this one last difficulty. Sometimes I would give way to wild outbursts of rage, and hack and splinter some unlucky tree in my intolerable vexation. But I could think of nothing.

And then came a day, a wonderful day, that I spent in ecstasy. I saw a sail to the southwest, a small sail like that of a little schooner, and forthwith I lit a great pile of brushwood and stood by it in the heat of it and the heat of the midday sun, watching. All day I watched that sail, eating or drinking nothing, so that my head reeled; and the Beasts came and glared at me, and seemed to wonder, and went away. The boat was still distant when night came and swallowed it up, and all night I toiled to keep my blaze bright and high, and the eyes of the Beasts shone out of the darkness, marvelling. In the dawn it was nearer, and I saw it was the dirty lug-sail of a small boat. My eyes were weary with watching, and I peered and could not believe them. Two men were in the boat, sitting low down, one by the bows and the other at the rudder. But the boat sailed strangely. The head was not kept to the wind; it yawed and fell away.

As the day grew brighter I began waving the last rag of my jacket to them; but they did not notice me, and sat still facing one another. I went to the lowest point of the low headland and gesticulated and shouted. There was no response, and the boat kept on her aimless course, making slowly, very slowly, for the bay. Suddenly a great white bird flew up out of the boat, and neither of the men stirred nor noticed it. It circled round, and then came sweeping overhead with its strong wings outspread.

Then I stopped shouting, and sat down on the headland and rested my chin on my hands and stared. Slowly, slowly, the boat drove past towards the west. I would have swum out to it, but something, a cold vague fear, kept me back. In the afternoon the tide stranded it, and left it a hundred yards or so to the westward of the ruins of the enclosure.

The men in it were dead, had been dead so long that they fell to pieces when I tilted the boat on its side and dragged them out. One had a shock of red hair like the captain of the

Ipecacuanha, and a dirty white cap lay in the bottom of the boat. As I stood beside the boat, three of the Beasts came slinking out of the bushes and sniffing towards me. One of my spasms of disgust came upon me. I thrust the little boat down the beach and clambered on board her. Two of the brutes were Wolf Beasts, and came forward with quivering nostrils and glittering eyes; the third was the horrible nondescript of bear and bull.

When I saw them approaching those wretched remains, heard them snarling at one another, and caught the gleam of their teeth, a frantic horror succeeded my repulsion. I turned my back upon them, struck the lug, and began paddling out to sea. I could not bring myself to look behind me.

But I lay between the reef and the island that night, and the next morning went round to the stream and filled the empty keg aboard with water. Then, with such patience as I could command, I collected a quantity of fruit, and waylaid and killed two rabbits with my last three cartridges. While I was doing this I left the boat moored to an inward projection of the reef, for fear of the Beast Monsters.

22

The Man alone

In the evening I started and drove out to sea before a gentle wind from the south-west, slowly and steadily, and the island grew smaller and smaller, and the lank spire of smoke dwindled to a finer and finer line against the hot sunset. The ocean rose up around me, hiding that low dark patch from my eyes. The daylight, the trailing glory of the sun, went streaming out of the sky, was drawn aside like some luminous curtain, and at last I looked into that blue gulf of immensity that the sunshine hides, and saw the floating hosts of the stars. The sea was silent, the sky was silent; I was alone with the night and silence.

So I drifted for three days, eating and drinking sparingly, and meditating upon all that happened to me, nor desiring very greatly then to see men again. One unclean rag was about me, my hair a black tangle. No doubt my discoverers thought me a madman. It is strange, but I felt no desire to return to mankind. I was only glad to be quit of the foulness of the Beast Monsters. And on the third day I was picked up by a brig from Apia to San Francisco. Neither the captain nor the mate would believe my story, judging that solitude and danger had made me mad. And fearing their opinion might be that of others, I refrained from telling my adventure further, and professed to recall nothing that had happened to me between the loss of the *Lady Vain* and the time when I was picked up again – the space of a year.

I had to act with the utmost circumspection to save myself from the suspicion of insanity. My memory of the Law, of the two dead sailors, of the ambuscades of the darkness, of the body in the cane brake, haunted me. And, unnatural as it seems, with my return to mankind came, instead of that confidence and sympathy I had expected, a strange enhancement of the uncertainty and dread I had experienced during my stay upon the island. No one would believe me, I was almost as queer to men as I had been to the Beast People. I may have caught something of the natural wildness of my companions.

They say that terror is a disease, and anyhow, I can witness that, for several years now, a restless fear has dwelt in my mind, such a restless fear as a half-tamed lion cub may feel. My trouble took the strangest form. I could not persuade myself that the men and women I met were not also another, still passably human, Beast People, animals half-wrought into the outward image of human souls, and that they would presently begin to revert, to show first this bestial mark and then that. But I have confided my case to a strangely able man, a man who had known Moreau, and seemed half to credit my story, a mental specialist – and he has helped me mightily.

Though I do not expect that the terror of that island will ever altogether leave me, at most times it lies far in the back of my mind, a mere distant cloud, a memory and a faint distrust; but there are times when the little cloud spreads until it obscures the whole sky. Then I look about me at my fellow-men. And I go in fear. I see faces keen and bright, others dull or dangerous, others unsteady, insincere; none that have the calm authority of a reasonable soul. I feel as though the animal was surging up through them; that presently the degradation of the Islanders will be played over again on a larger scale. I know this is an illusion, that these seeming men and women about me are indeed men and women, men and women for ever, perfectly reasonable creatures, full of human desires and tender solicitude, emancipated from instinct, and the slaves of no fantastic Law – beings altogether different from the Beast Folk. Yet I shrink from them, from their curious glances, their inquiries and assistance, and long to be away from them and alone.

For that reason I live near the broad free downland, and can escape thither when this shadow is over my soul; and very sweet is the empty downland then, under the wind-swept sky. When I lived in London the horror was wellnigh insupportable. I could not get away from men; their voices came through windows; locked doors were flimsy safeguards. I would go out into the streets to fight with my delusion, and prowling women would mew after me, furtive craving men glanced jealously at me, weary pale workers go coughing by me, with tired eyes and eager paces like wounded deer dripping blood, old people, bent and dull, pass murmuring to themselves, and all unheeding a ragged tail of gibing children. Then I would turn aside into some chapel, and even there, such was my disturbance, it seemed that the preacher gibbered Big Thinks even as the Ape Man had done; or into some library, and there the intent faces over the books seemed but patient creatures waiting for prey. Particularly nauseous were the blank expressionless faces of people in trains and omnibuses; they seemed no more my fellow-creatures than dead bodies would be, so that I did not dare to travel unless I was assured of being alone. And even it seemed that I, too, was not a reasonable creature, but only an animal tormented with some strange disorder in its brain, that sent it to wander alone, like a sheep stricken with the gid.

But this is a mood that comes to me now – I thank God – more rarely. I have withdrawn myself from the confusion of cities and multitudes, and spend my days surrounded by wise books, bright windows in this life of ours lit by the shining souls of men. I see few strangers, and have but a small household. My days I devote to reading and to experiments in chemistry, and I spend many of the clear nights in the study of astronomy. There is, though I do not know how there is or why there is, a sense of infinite peace and protection in the glittering hosts of heaven. There it must be, I think, in the vast and eternal laws of matter, and not in the daily cares and sins and troubles of men, that whatever is more than animal within us must find its solace and its hope. I hope, or I could not live. And so, in hope and solitude, my story ends.

Edward Prendick.

H. G. WELLS AND HIS CRITICS

[The sufferings of the Beast People had] absolutely no artistic reason. [The] disgusting descriptions arouse loathing without any equivalent personal interest.

The Athenaeum

A more gruesomely grotesque and uncanny tale . . . it would be hard to imagine.

The Critic

A morbid aberration of scientific curiosity.

Daily Telegraph

Only an extreme instance of the horrible, the weird and the uncanny which characterise all his writings.

Review of Reviews

Mr Wells seems to us to have allowed his imagination too free a run in his new story.

Natural Science

The strong reactionary effect which is produced at the close of the story and the terrible fate which is meted out to the impiously daring vivisectionalist are the saving points of the book.

The Critic

An atrocious miracle.

Jorge Luis Borges

The youthful exuberance of these passages is as notable as their pungency. Wells was playing the melodramatic role of *enfant terrible* assaulting the complacency of late Victorian society.

Patrick Parrinder, *H. G. Wells*, 1970

The novel develops a symmetrical system in which for every symbolic link between human and beast there is a symbolic separation, and often the very terms of union contain within them the seeds of division.

John Huntington, *The Logic of Fantasy: H. G. Wells and Science Fiction*, 1982

SUGGESTIONS FOR FURTHER READING

H. G. Wells, *The Time Machine*, 1895
—, *The War of the Worlds*, 1897
—, *The Invisible Man*, 1897
—, *Mankind in the Making*, 1903
Norman and Jeanne Mackenzie, *The Time Traveller: The Life of H. G. Wells*, 1973
Roslynn D. Haynes, *H. G. Wells: Discoverer of the Future: The Influence of Science on his Thought*, 1980
Brian W. Aldiss, *Moreau's Other Island*, 1980
—, with David Wingrove, *Trillion Year Spree: The History of Science Fiction*, 1986
Patrick Parrinder and Christopher Rolphe (eds), *H. G. Wells Under Revision*, 1990

The Comprehensive Bibliography of H. G. Wells's work, compiled by the H. G. Wells Society (Fourth Edition 1986) lists 154 books (including novels) and pamphlets by Wells, about 80 short stories, and a number of posthumous works.

TEXT SUMMARY

Introduction
Charles Prendick sets down the facts, such as they are, concerning his uncle's disappearance and rescue.

1 *In the Dingey of the 'Lady Vain'*
Following the sinking of the 'Lady Vain', Edward Prendick drifts for days without food or water, but is rescued.

2 *The Man who was Going Nowhere*
Aboard the 'Ipecacuanha', Prendick is cared for by Montgomery; he hears strange growling noises coming from the deck.

3 *The Strange Face*
Prendick meets a grotesque, deformed creature; on the ship's deck he finds dogs, rabbits, a llama and a puma; he also witnesses an argument between Montgomery and the ship's drunk captain.

4 *At the Schooner's Rail*
Prendick is curious about Montgomery and his menagerie; Montgomery seems on the point of telling him a long-held secret, but refrains.

5 *The Man who had Nowhere to go*
Arriving at their destination, Montgomery and his animals are met by an elderly, white-haired gentleman. The captain insists Prendick leave the ship with them, but the white-haired gentleman refuses. Prendick is thrown into the dingey of the 'Lady Vain' and left to drift.

6 *The Evil-looking Boatmen*
Prendick is rescued by Montgomery and lands on the island. He wonders at the deformed shapes of the boatmen. The white-haired man becomes more welcoming.

7 The Locked Door
Prendick is shown to his quarters and wonders what is behind the door that is kept locked. Montgomery and the elderly man will not tell him. He hears Montgomery call the elderly man 'Moreau' and remembers the context in which he has heard the name before.

8 The Crying of the Puma
Prendick quizzes Montgomery about his deformed attendant and the men on the beach, but is not given a satisfactory answer. All the while, the puma is screaming in pain.

9 The Thing in the Forest
To escape the puma's screams, Prendick sets out to explore the island. He comes across more deformed creatures, one of which follows him.

10 The Crying of the Man
Prendick hears human crying. He opens the door, which Montgomery had forgotten to lock, but is thrown back by Moreau.

11 The Hunting of the Man
Prendick escapes from the enclosure. He meets another Beast Man and follows him.

12 The Sayers of the Law
Prendick is taken by the Ape Man to the Beast People's village where he witnesses the chanting of their laws. Discovered by Moreau and Montgomery, he flees.

13 A Parley
Prendick is tracked down by Moreau and Montgomery and persuaded to return with them.

14 Doctor Moreau explains
Moreau tells Prendick of his life's work.

15 Concerning the Beast Folk
Prendick describes some of Moreau's 'creations'.

16 *How the Beast Folk Tasted Blood*
Montgomery is disturbed to discover the savaged corpse of a rabbit. Moreau summons the Beast People to find the culprit, who is then chased. Before Moreau can get his hands on it, Prendick kills it; he then reflects on the misery of the Beast People's existence.

17 *A Catastrophe*
The puma escapes; Moreau goes in pursuit and disappears. Montgomery goes after him, but returns empty handed.

18 *The Finding of Moreau*
Prendick and Montgomery go in search of Moreau. They find his body and bring it back to the enclosure; they then set fire to the laboratory.

19 *Montgomery's 'Bank Holiday'*
Lamenting his fate, Montgomery goes off for a last night of drunken revelry. He and his attendant are attacked by the Beast People.

20 *Alone with the Beast Folk*
Prendick orders the Beast Folk to get rid of Montgomery's body. He is threatened by the Hyaena-Swine.

21 *The Reversion of the Beast Folk*
Prendick spends ten months on the island, during which time the Beast Folk gradually lose their human characteristics. A ship runs aground on the island and Prendick prepares to escape.

22 *The Man alone*
Prendick is rescued and returns home, but his experiences have affected him greatly.

CLASSIC FICTION
IN EVERYMAN

The Impressions of Theophrastus Such
GEORGE ELIOT
An amusing collection of character sketches, and the only paperback edition available
£5.99

Frankenstein
MARY SHELLEY
A masterpiece of Gothic terror in its original 1818 version
£3.99

East Lynne
MRS HENRY WOOD
A classic tale of melodrama, murder and mystery
£7.99

Holiday Romance and Other Writings for Children
CHARLES DICKENS
Dickens's works for children, including 'The Life of Our Lord' and 'A Child's History of England', with original illustrations
£5.99

The Ebb-Tide
R. L. STEVENSON
A compelling study of ordinary people in extreme circumstances
£4.99

The Three Impostors
ARTHUR MACHEN
The only edition available of this cult thriller
£4.99

Mister Johnson
JOYCE CARY
The only edition available of this amusing but disturbing twentieth-century tale
£5.99

The Jungle Book
RUDYARD KIPLING
The classic adventures of Mowgli and his friends
£3.99

Glenarvon
LADY CAROLINE LAMB
The only edition available of the novel which throws light on the greatest scandal of the early nineteenth century – the infatuation of Caroline Lamb with Lord Byron
£6.99

Twenty Thousand Leagues Under the Sea
JULES VERNE
Scientific fact combines with fantasy in this prophetic tale of underwater adventure
£4.99

All books are available from your local bookshop or direct from:
Littlehampton Book Services Cash Sales, 14 Eldon Way, Lineside Estate,
Littlehampton, West Sussex BN17 7HE (*prices are subject to change*)

To order any of the books, please enclose a cheque (in sterling) made payable to
Littlehampton Book Services, or phone your order through with credit card details (Access,
Visa or Mastercard) on 01903 721596 (24 hour answering service) stating card number
and expiry date. (*Please add £1.25 for package and postage to the total of your order.*)

In the USA, for further information and a complete catalogue call 1-800-526-2778